How You Lead
and Manage

Define – Document – Clarify – Refine™

Dwaine Canova

i

Also, by Dwaine Canova

Overcoming the Four Deceptions:
In Career Relationships

A *Framework for Leading*™ Series

Improve leading and managing in your organization.

Books:

1 – A Framework for Leading™:
Simple – Easy – Effective
(Building a Foundation)

2 – A Framework for Leading™:
The Top Level
(Elevate Your View)

3 – A Framework for Leading™:
Advantages
(A Managing Methodology for Leaders)

4 – A Framework for Leading™:
Expectations and Outcomes
(Anticipate and Innovate)

5 – A Framework for Leading™:
Connect and Align
(Communicating in High-Performance Organizations)

6 – A Framework for Leading™:
Strategic Initiatives
(Create, Prioritize, and Execute Strategies)

More books are coming in this series …

How You Lead and Manage

Define – Document – Clarify – Refine™

Printed by CreateSpace.com
Printed in the United States of America
ISBN-13: 978-1987478020
ISBN-10: 1987478029

CreateSpace Independent Publishing Platform
North Charleston, South Carolina

Illustrations: Shanna and Joseph Morehouse of StarSite Media, LLC
Cover: Andrew Pinch and Chris Danner of Printing Solutions, LLC

The websites included in this book are presented as a resource to the reader. This is not meant to imply an endorsement, nor can we vouch for their content for the life of this book.

All trademarked items as noted with a (™) in this book are the property of Dwaine Canova or Zynity, LLC, unless otherwise noted. All other trademarks used herein are property of their respective owners.

Dwaine's Mission: Serving* Leaders and Managers

*Serving is helping, responding, anticipating,
and encouraging with full attention to another's best interests.

To

Robert H. Breinholt, PhD

professor, partner, mentor, friend

Contents

In a Nutshell 3

The Challenge 5

Your Story 12

The Template (Create your document)....... 14

    1. Philosophy…..................................... 18

    2. What We Do…................................ 24

    3. The Markets We Serve.................... 41

    4. Our Organization........................... 48

    5. New Ways and New Things 64

    6. Being Customer Focused 76

    7. Eyes on the Numbers 85

    8. Resources…… 105

Do It Your Way 119

You Know It's Working When… 123

Apply What You Document 125

Grow and Develop 132

Leadership Styles 138

Growth Stages 141

The Online Tools 152

The Methodology 158

Additional Thoughts 162

Acknowledgments 180

The Author 183

Every now and then,
maybe once in a hundred cases,
a new idea turns out to be
on the mark, valid, and wonderful.

—Carl Sagan

In a Nutshell

This is written for leaders and managers who are passionately committed to improving their abilities. It introduces a process to help you on your journey.

The book takes you through a fun and beneficial process to write your own *'How I Lead and Manage'* document. A special web page[1] (no fee), along with this book, guides you, at your own pace, in a simple, step-by-step process. The output is your own treatise[2] of leadership.

Your organization's performance will improve. Your relationships and interactions will be more effective. New levels of respect and trust will be gained. You'll establish a more defined leading and managing system allowing your organization to thrive.

It's not about learning new things. You already know significantly more about leading and managing than you apply. This process helps you organize what you already know so you apply your knowledge more effectively.

Your treatise[2] becomes the solid foundation you add upon to continue clarifying and refining how you lead and manage. Your new understandings and insights about yourself and leadership will improve your life.

This will inspire those around you to join in the same journey. Collaborating with others helps everyone.

Enjoy!

---

[1] www.Zynity.com go to the link ***How You Lead*** to get started when you're ready.

[2] Treatise /'trēdis/ a written work dealing formally and systematically with a subject.

People of accomplishment rarely sat back and let things happen to them. They went out and happened to things.

—Leonardo da Vinci

The Challenge

What is your answer to the following question?

How do you lead and manage?

Very few leaders and managers have been asked this question. So, if you don't immediately have a clear reply, don't fret. Very few of your peers have a compact and clear answer. The challenge: create your answer.

The purpose of this book is twofold:

(1) Explain and illustrate why it's necessary to have a ready answer.
(2) Guide you to create your own clear answer.

Having a ready answer is necessary for two reasons:

(1) Your clear answer makes it easier for others to engage actively (teach, learn, and collaborate) with your leading and managing beliefs and style.
(2) Once you have it, it's easier to grow and refine it on an ongoing basis.

The following is assumed about those reading this book:

(1) You look for ways to improve.
(2) You know it takes small steps to make leaps.
(3) You enjoy learning.
(4) You learn faster by doing.

This book guides you in a process to create your clear and compact expression of how you lead and manage. It also encourages you to involve others in your process and journey to continue evolving and refining.

Expressing your *how* clearly, must include, the way you speak it, write it, and execute it. This is a foundation for scalable leadership. Scaling means increasing your capabilities and capacities as you and your role change.

Special note: In this book we present leading and managing together often. They are different, but individuals in leadership and management roles perform both leading and managing activities in an intertwined way. It's almost impossible to do one without including the other. *Leading* is most simply defined as a focus on the future to ensure the organization is doing the right things. *Managing* is most simply defined as a focus on the present to ensure individuals are doing things right.

The overall objective is to create an environment in which the talented individuals in your organization can collaborate, contribute, and flourish together. More about the specifics of an environment are coming in a moment.

Your way of leading and managing has four distinct dimensions:

(1) Purpose – Includes both your *why* and *what* you expect to accomplish.
(2) Clarity – May be assessed by how well those around you understand all you think, say, and do.
(3) Framework – The structure within which you define, clarify, refine, and build your system.
(4) Environment – The features within your sphere that describe what it's like to live in your system.

Purpose

It helps to describe specifics about why you want to lead, how you go about it, and what you expect to accomplish. This should include a summary and high-level expression of your motives and your attitudes about your role and the resources it engages. This requires the fewest words but the deepest insights. It's about who you are and what you want to contribute.

Clarity

Everyone has a system for *how* they lead and manage. It's not usually clearly understood and articulated by the leader or those around them. Your system is comprised of many details and nuances required for your organization to function. It's difficult to describe in simple terms.

The guidance in this book adds significant clarity for everyone's system. The effort is not about changing your system. The effort is about documenting and applying it in a manner that gets you to clarity as well as all those needing and wanting to engage with you. After getting clarity then you can make selected adjustments as seems appropriate.

It's essential to understand the importance of my often-repeated statement: *In all great things, the magnificence is in the details.* It's always the details that separate the greats from the goods. Clarity is achieved through attention to the details.

Framework

The framework is an outline of all the big dimensions of a system. In this book, we establish the framework as consisting of these four dimensions:

(1) Managing Team – Connected and aligned
(2) Strategies – Create, prioritize, and implement
(3) Customers – Focus and leverage roles to serve
(4) Measurements – Numerical and other outcomes

It's important that every leader be able to answer the following four questions with specifics and confidence:

(1) How do you make sure your leading and managing team members are connected and working in alignment with one another?
(2) How do you create strategic initiatives, clarify their expectations, prioritize them, and execute them in the right priority and time frame?
(3) How do you make certain all individuals know how they're supposed to be customer focused and how their part adds to the customer's experience?
(4) How do you know you're measuring and managing the right things, and attention to the measurements is creating the results you desire?

There are many details in each of the above four dimensions, but we know almost every detail of the organization fits within one of these four dimensions. Conceptually it's easy to discuss each one without having to include all the details. Also, by having clarity about each of these at the conceptual level, it's easier to ensure the details fit and work together within the dimension.

Environment

The environment is created by the following four items:

(1) Content – An organization's information
(2) Lexicon – Word use in a common language
(3) Culture – Concepts and principles guiding behavior and decisions
(4) Interactions – The parts working together in harmony

Content is all the information used and shared for leading and managing thinking and activities.

Lexicon is the specific and disciplined use of words, within an organization, which may be the same or somewhat different than their dictionary definition.

Culture encompasses thinking, behaviors, attitudes, motives, and beliefs. Each one is usually described in concepts and principles. *Concepts* are clear and general ideas encompassing a broad and higher-level perspective of the whole. A broad and higher-level view allows individuals to create thinking and business rules that provide guidance about details in a variety of circumstances. Developing a broad and high-level perspective must be done intentionally. *Principles* are fundamental truths that apply in many situations. These establish the foundation upon which a framework and the system within can be established. Defining and clarifying your principles about culture must be done deliberately.

Interactions in an organization can't be accomplished well with just an elaborate and specific set of do-and-don't rules. Yes, there must be do and don't rules for many things. They can't be expected to cover every activity or event. There must be a clear set of guiding concepts and principles for individuals to adapt, change, accommodate the new, and adjust as needed to change.

We live in a world of greater and faster rates of change than ever before. Clarity about concepts and principles (which also must adapt and change) allow talented individuals to create and input their own do-and-don't insights as-they-go that fit within the organization's environment. This establishes an environment that encourages agile, responsive, innovative decisions, and behaviors allowing growth and flourishing for individuals. This encourages maturing and scaling of the organization and individuals. It makes it much easier for growing entities to onboard, incorporate, and engage new employees as well as adapt and morph roles of existing individuals.

Your Story

Having clarity for you and others, about the above, is accomplished by creating your own document including each of the dimensions described above. This makes it possible for you and others to read it, discuss it, explain it, add to it, and keep refining it. It quickly becomes your foundation for clarifying your thinking and behaving within defined and clear concepts and principles.

The challenge is: Will you take the time (at your own pace) to create your clear and compact answer?

For the things we have to learn
before we can do them,
we learn by doing them.

—Aristotle

Your Story

How you lead and manage is a dynamic story. It's your story. The many things you think, say, and do today as a leader and manager are important. They evolve over time. Yes, do it your way, but remember it's all about how it relates to and impacts the lives of others.

The ability to explain clearly how you lead and manage will set you apart from your peers. If all the leaders and managers within your organization can explain theirs, it will be easier for you to respect, understand, and work effectively with each other.

There is a large body of knowledge and many opinions suggesting the dysfunction, distractions, and poor performance of organizations is due to less than optimal leading and managing. Teams work hard but with less success than their efforts deserve.

The fix for this begins with each of us establishing clarity about how we lead and manage. Write your story so you and your team will work smarter, be more effective, and accomplish more in an environment noted for its harmony.

Make your story better every day!

We are what we repeatedly do.
Excellence, then, is not an act,
but a habit.

—Aristotle

The Template (Create your document)

How You Lead and Manage

A brief overview of the outline

Defining and clarifying are essential to establish repeatable, successful, and transparent leadership. The process of creating your own version of your "How You Lead and Manage" document begins with completing the following outline with your thoughts and ideas. Access to a special web page is available, for your personal use, on Zynity's home page at www.Zynity.com.

Following is a picture of the big link located on the right side as you scroll down Zynity's home page. Click on this link, register, and get started. There is no cost.

Use the information in this book to help you complete your personal document. This is for use by principal leaders and leaders/managers of departments in all types of organizations.

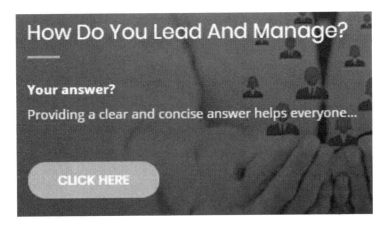

Once at the website, simply click as indicated and you'll be guided to start the process. Start with writing a sentence or two in each of the sections below. Add your content as needed. It grows quickly. You create focus and clarity with each step. Don't rush. Do a little each week.

Spend time with others detecting and reflecting when you're leading and when you're managing. Be careful not to excuse yourself from leading by spending so much time managing. You must do both intentionally to build a strong organization. The right amount of each will depend on your stage of development (organizational and personal), your resources, and the present and coming circumstances.

Following is the outline for this book and your document. I provide examples for you within each section using actual information from my company, Zynity, LLC:

1. Philosophy
   a. Key words
   b. Theme
   c. Leadership statement

2. What we do
   a. Why we do it
   b. Description
   c. How we do it
   d. Core competencies
   e. The problem we solve

3. The markets we serve
   a. Descriptions
   b. What we deliver

4. Our Organization
    a. Chart
    b. Character, culture, and core values
    c. Working together effectively and efficiently

5. New ways and new things
    a. Opportunities and innovations
    b. Prioritizing and implementing strategic initiatives

6. Everyone customer focused at all times
    a. Categories
    b. Keeping the customer's view

7. Eyes on the numbers in all parts
    a. Budgets and goals
    b. Key Performance Metrics (KPMs)
    c. Measuring to grow and improve

8. Resources
    a. Capital
    b. Individuals
    c. Processes
    d. Technology
    e. Outside professionals

You must be intentional with your leading and managing. This small document you're creating will help you in this process.

Philosophy, rightly defined, is simply the love of wisdom.

—Marcus Tullius Cicero

1. Philosophy

High-level and broad thinking

Creating a personal leading and managing philosophy requires broad, high-level thinking. A philosophy can be concisely expressed in three ways:

(1) Key words
(2) A theme
(3) A statement

These three ways form a complete expression of a leading and managing philosophy. It can be shared in a few words or a few short paragraphs. All three versions of the philosophy are useful and appropriate in very different circumstances. Our ability to use all three equips us for all occasions.

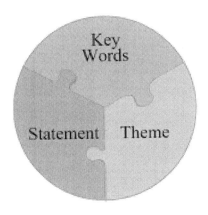

Establishing and defining your philosophy about how you lead and manage is an important first step. It will provide the necessary foundation to distinguish your leading and managing methodology. It's a way of presenting, in a concise form, connected concepts to cover a broad area of many specific things. This includes the expected outcomes and guiding principles used to get things done.

Following are the key words I use. This expresses my philosophy in a few words. This makes it easier for everyone to remember and share. These words are used often daily.

a. Key words

Purpose – Clarity – Focus – Structure

Following is how this looks at the website. We have this one sample of how it looks at the website to make it familiar when you get to the website. It's just this simple. A text box for you to input your text. It looks something like this. (Website geniuses will continue refining this.)

Philosophy

a. Key words

```
┌──────────────────────────────────────────────┐
│  Purpose – Clarity – Focus – Structure       │
└──────────────────────────────────────────────┘
```

It's as simple as the above. A title for the box and you input your text. No whistles, no bells, just your knowledge and heart in one box of text at a time.

This is a general reminder for the process and the rest of your boxes. You build your document one section at a time. In your process, you'll likely have some boxes begin with only a word or two and then come back later and grow them to a sentence. You will come back later and grow those to a paragraph or two and even add illustrations or drawings. It's yours. Do with it as you wish. (Okay I sneaked in a line from one of my favorite movies.)

Now, let's build a theme to expand on the words. I use this to express more fully my attitudes, motives, and emotions.

b. Theme

Passion, compassion, communication within an operating system, so everyone is getting better every day.

Okay, following is one more example of how this looks on the website. Again, it's just this simple. A text box for you to input your text. It looks something like this.

It's as simple as the above. A title for the box and you input your text. Notice the box expands to accept all the text and illustrations you want. No whistles, no bells, just your knowledge and heart in one box of text at a time.

Following is the more elaborate explanation (statement) to use when more detail is needed. This statement amplifies the theme and gives more detail about our guidelines and principles. It's for those wanting to hear more.

c. Statement

> Provide a simple, clear, and focused presentation of the organization and its purpose. Establish strategies and a framework for leading and managing to engage each person in their role to amplify their contributions and sense of personal value. They can then work together better.
>
> Attract, select, and nurture spectacular individuals to participate in refining and exceeding what the organization is expected to accomplish for everyone in its world. Encourage everyone to be fanatics about serving and providing value to customers as well as all our stakeholders.
>
> Get the big parts working together seamlessly and pay careful attention to all the important details. Motivate everyone to get better every day.

The above text can be edited and updated at any time. It's recommended the various revisions and additions be dated and saved for later review and reference. A stroll through the changes is a fun journey to obtain insights about trends and progress with your thinking.

Creating your own philosophy forces you to think at a conceptual level. This opens one to think more broadly and deeply about all they do from a higher-level perspective. Many good things will become obvious as you have exposure to the process and experience.

Summary

Expressing your leading and managing philosophy simply and fully is necessary to convey your clarity about *what* you are doing and *how* you are doing it. This high-level perspective helps all stakeholders understand the general guidelines, principles, and heart you use to lead and manage your organization.

You will be infinitely more successful if you contribute to the success of others.

—Ann Marie Houghtailing

2. What We Do

Our value to others

Life should be centered around what we contribute to others. Carefully defining your value to others is an essential early-stage step.

Before I describe *what* we do, let me explain *why* we create and deploy online tools and a methodology to bring clarity to our leading and managing. Our motives help expresses our heart and passion for what we do.

a. Why we do what we do

I'm intrigued and influenced by the work of Simon Sinek and his book, *Start with Why.*

I like:
- Its popularity
- Its cleverness
- Its reasonable explanations
- Its community of followers
- Its focus on "what's greater than me" to inspire individuals

Simon Sinek's example of *why* for Apple Inc. is:

"Everything we do we believe in challenging the status quo. We believe in thinking differently. The way we challenge the status quo is by making our products beautifully designed, simple to use and user friendly. And we happen to make great computers. Wanna buy one?"

The summary is:

> **Why?** – Challenge the status quo and think differently
> **How?** – Make our products beautifully designed, simple to use, and user friendly
> **What?** – Great computers

And now for Zynity.

> **Our *why* for the *Framework for Leading*™ and *Zynity Leadership*™ (ZL) online tools is:**

"In all we do, we believe in celebrating the high worth of individuals. We believe in creating harmony. We create it through our leading and managing designed to help individuals work together better. We provide great and easy-to-use concepts, courses, and online tools.
Wanna buy our methodology, books, courses, online tools, and coaches?"

The summary is:

> **Why?** – Create vibrant and rewarding *life* in thriving organizations
> **How?** – Establish a motivating and productive leading and managing environment
> **What?** – Methodology, books, courses, online tools, and coaches

b. Description of what we do

We provide a solution to make leading and managing scalable. It includes a set of online tools, a methodology, books, courses, and a network of certified coaches. The capabilities are useful whether the subscribing organization employs ten or one thousand individuals. We contribute to the quality of life and success of organizations and the individuals in those organizations.

c. How we do what we do

The business model is a web-based platform offered in a Software as a Service (SaaS) option. Our solution is accessible through our website at www.Zynity.com. The basic unit of business (who we ask to pay), the elements of our operating infrastructure, and growth mechanisms are listed below.

Basic unit of business:
Subscribers

Infrastructure elements:
Organization
Website
Book series
Online courses
Certified Coach Network
Webinars
Seminars
Contact center
Alliance partners

26

Growth mechanisms:
>Alliances
>Referral sources
>Social media
>Public relations
>Marketing
>Sales (tele-sales and direct)
>Certified Coach Network

Listing the above major ingredients is necessary to help explain your organization and how it's designed to make all the right things happen daily. The **basic unit of business** defines the element(s) with which we create revenue. If we were an automobile dealership it would be cars sold and a second one would be cars serviced. The **infrastructure elements** are the items required for us to conduct our business. The **growth mechanisms** highlight the major channels used to create new business as well as nurture relationships with existing customers.

Staying closely connected with customers helps identify new opportunities for product/service development and enhancements. Understanding how your products and services add value to your customers' lives creates distinct advantages for your organization.

d. Core competencies

Our core competencies are the defining capabilities and qualities that distinguish us as an organization. They are the capabilities we amplify to give us a competitive advantage and successes in the marketplace. They allow us to bring value to our customers and the things we become known for within the community. Following is our list (which we refine and edit from time to time):

Leadership
Management
Training
Communication
Online tools
Learning
Empowering others
Collaboration
Planning
Strategies
Implementing
Entrepreneurial attitude
Research
Innovation

e. The problem we solve

A great way to share your story is to create a video or slide show addressing the big issues in the industry or community in which you do business. The following is a slide show with commentary we use to explain the problem we're solving and how we bring value to the community. Our community is small and midsize companies as well as parts of larger companies.

Following is our presentation in slide form. Beneath each slide is the narrative explanation of the points in the slides. We use this to explain *why* we are doing *what* we do, *how* we do it, and the value provided. We use this to explain us to all stakeholders, community, vendors, and clients who have an interest in *what* we do. Almost everyone in our organization is more than capable of using this slide show in a presentation format with a single person or group of people.

Slide #1

A Big Need

More thriving businesses

The need for more thriving businesses is universal. Every city, state, and country are eager for more companies to flourish so they can be contributors to their communities economically and socially.

Slide # 2

The Problem

Growing a thriving business isn't easy!

Building and growing a business that lasts and thrives over the years is difficult to accomplish. Failures and struggling organizations are symptoms of the difficulty.

Slide #3

Proof of the Problem

- 25% fail in the first year
- 55% fail by the 5th year
- 70% fail by the 10th year

Source: US Small Business Administration

- 75% of VC-funded businesses do not create a return to their investors

Source: Shikar Ghosh, a senior lecturer at Harvard Business School

---

The failure statistics itemized above have remained steady for a few decades. It seems the news sources present mostly the success stories, so the public isn't generally aware of these opportunities for improvement.

I suspect every one of the failures included very determined, hardworking, talented, and committed people. It isn't easy to build and grow a thriving business with a new idea or even an established idea. It's complicated. There are many moving parts and all the parts are moving all the time. Change and adaptation are two positive and negative ongoing influences. We feel that establishing definition and clarity with our leading and managing helps organizations change and adapt more easily and effectively.

Slide #4

Consider these positives in recent years:

- Thousands of management books
- Thousands of leadership books
- Millions of PhDs, MBAs, BAs
- Seminars, webinars, training

All very high quality

There are millions of positive things going on in the leading and managing community. The books and individuals are of incredibly high-quality. There is an abundance of great thinking, writing, and teaching.

There are also many other very good things going on to help businesses grow and thrive; The Small Business Administration, The Small Business Development Corporation, universities, colleges, incubators, accelerators, consulting groups, etc.

We bring to this great mix a practical methodology and online tools to help people apply more easily and effectively what they learn and know in community with others.

Slide #5

```
                    Questions

    •  Why are the failure stats not
       improving?
    •  What can be done to improve the
       statistics?
```

There are many, and no, simple answers. We've spent
some time exploring answers to these two questions and
we begin answering them in the next slides.

Slide #6

```
                   Two Solutions

    •  Better business ideas
    •  Better implementation

    Our focus is:
       Better implementation
```

Better ideas are not the opportunity we're addressing.
There appear to be plenty of very good ideas already and
many more will surely appear. We want to help more of
the ideas get implemented properly so the organizations
can thrive. It begins with leading and managing.

Our focus is on what can be done better to improve implementation. Leaders and managers are very good about acquiring new knowledge and skills, yet they struggle to implement these new things into their organizations. Why are adopting and implementing these new things so difficult?

Leaders and managers are not usually as systematic in their leading and managing as they are in their daily operations. It's hard for them to apply their new knowledge about leading and managing without an established structure in place.

Some companies use such disciplines as Six Sigma to improve the processes in their operating activities. Some companies use online automation tools to improve their project management and sales activities. Very few use the discipline of processes and online tools in their leading and managing. This is the opportunity we present to increase the rate of implementation success.

Slide #7

Leaders can be helped if they:

- Are coachable
- Are willing to add clarity
- Will adopt new disciplines
- Can adopt new technologies

Becoming more systematic with leading and managing engages the whole leading and managing team in the process. This enhances the culture and operating environment within which they work.

Slide #8

The Opportunity

Defined leadership:

- Brings clarity
- Ensures focus
- Increases performance
- Reduces stress
- Increases engagement

A more defined and clarified environment makes it easier and more positive to work within. There is an added connectedness that incites awareness of what others are doing and makes it acceptable to give encouragement and acknowledgement in a manner that's very effective. The impact of the quick reply or comment is felt by all within the team. Individuals enjoy seeing others recognized for many reasons.

The ZL online tools facilitate this sharing while avoiding email confusion. Also, the tools keep this sharing by topic in a journal for later reference.

Think back to all the emails received last week. Could you make decisions today with the comfort you have all the relevant input from the related stakeholders? Also consider, if one of the contributor/stakeholders left the organization, how much of their input would you retain and where would you find the email?

Slide #9

Role Models

Successful sports coaches
Create, define, and evolve
their own system …

… to get teams performing
at very high levels.

We need to do the same!

The use of coaches as examples is appropriate because so many leaders and managers are sports fans. Most have a favorite team and/or coach they admire. Their coaches are noted and celebrated for having a system to lead and manage their teams. Most leaders and managers don't have a celebrated and cherished leading and managing system yet. We hope to change that with this leadership methodology, this book, and the online tools.

Slide #10

Step One

Creating clarity begins
with defining a framework.

It begins with a few baby steps. Overcoming inertia and the thought that we haven't needed this before are two early barriers. Those who need it the least are usually the first to get new things underway. Our solution is a set of steps we guide each one through to create their own framework in a manner and style that works for them.

Slide #11

Create leadership alignment...

- *Zynity Leadership*™ *(ZL)*
  online tools

    Combined with:

- *A Framework for Leading*™
  methodology with online training

    Combined with:

- *ZL's Certified Coaches* network

36

The above three items in Slide #11 are the core pieces of our offering/solution. They are designed to be used together for maximum results.

The *Zynity Leadership*™ (ZL) online tools provide the organization a place to house and use their leading and managing information. Once in the tools, they can use their information more effectively. To help you relate to this, consider how much more effectively information for project managing is used once it's in an online tool.

Consider the same type of dynamic which occurs when sales and marketing information are placed in online tools. The access to and ability to work with information transforms how the related work gets done. This same transformation occurs when the leading and managing information is placed in the *Zynity Leadership*™ (ZL) online tools.

The *Framework for Leading*™ methodology and the ZL online tools are designed to work together. The methodology teaches how to build and implement a framework within which the organization's leading and managing team can build their own system. The methodology guides in knowing which information to include in the system and how to use it once it's in the online tools. It can be learned through the books and the related online training certification courses. The online courses are for individual users as well as the coaches.

The *Zynity Leadership*™ network of coaches facilitates the use of the methodology and the online tools. They bring their years of experience to help each organization improve their performance and their work culture.

Slide #12

Methodology and Online Tools

The benefits are …

- Establish definition for leadership
- Help the parts work together better
- Build a learning environment
- Provide a technology platform
- Increase productivity – performance

… everyone works better in harmony.

Our offering creates the above value points for our customers and the community at large. These are the benefits created when organizations apply our full solution. Without a solution, such as the one we're offering, there is more opportunity for chaos, dysfunction, added stress, and reduced productivity. Details about how to use the methodology and the online tools are not presented in this chapter. Nor will your document include a full demonstration of your product or service in this section.

The entire slide show (these twelve slides) is available to share with all stakeholders in the organization. This is our story and it's your way of telling your story. This is the core around which the organization is built. We refine this presentation continually. All changes and additions to the organization should begin with a clear understanding of the story and how each individual contribution will impact the story.

The value an organization creates for its community is a great source of joy and inspiration for all its stakeholders. Recognizing and celebrating the contributions is important for all parties and builds stronger individual engagement.

Has this section helped you better understand our organization? Does it encourage you to want a clearer understanding of yours?

Summary

It's critical to have and share clear messages about:
- the value you create for others
- what you do
- why you do it
- how you do it
- your core competencies

It's your story of the organization and the heart of who you are.

Taking time to document and continue refining the message about the organization will pay big dividends. It encourages, builds pride, and engages stakeholders with your current story and prepares them for next things.

The aim of marketing is to know and understand the customer so well the product or service fits him and sells itself.

—Peter Drucker

3. The Markets We Serve

Whom we seek to delight

We use the words **markets we serve** as a general pointer when discussing those for whom we provide value. Zynity's primary markets are small and midsize organizations. These are the individuals who pay us for what we deliver. Our focus is more about the individuals in our markets. We start with describing them in these following general terms.

We also have internal categories within our organization, such as fellow employees, vendors, and outside professionals. These are equally important markets (individuals) and we'll discuss more about them later.

a. Descriptions

Following is the list of details about our two categories of clients and customers. It includes demographic and psychographic information along with the decision makers and influencers. The purpose of this information is to make sure we understand their general characteristics and can express them in succinct terms. Our marketing and sales individuals add significant detail to this while working with individuals in each category of customers.

(1) Organizations:
- For profit and non-profit
- Stand alone or parts of other organizations

- 20+ employees with 3+ in the management team
- Growing in early stage through to mature
- Pre-starts and start-ups can also benefit from using the materials and tools

(2) Consultants, Coaches, Mentors (CCMs) (Certified Coaches):
- Individuals and companies
- Focus on small and midsize organizations (refer to above organization profile)
- Help in more than one functional area and connect at the leader level
- Who have 2+ years of consulting, coaching, or mentoring experience, or 10+ years executive experience

Profile for individuals in both groups:
- Use other online tools
- Use financials and reporting
- Use and understand the value of documented processes
- Innovators and learners
- Continuously improving
- Actively use short- and long-term goals

Buyers:
- Principal Leaders
- Functional Leaders

Influencers:
- Key Opinion Leaders (press, blogs, others)
- Principal Leaders' peers

- Functional Leaders and their peers
- Top functional area managers
- Coaches, consultants, and mentors
- Friends and associates

b. What We Deliver – Their Outcomes

Each category has different needs which defines what we must deliver for them.

(1) Organizations:

Following is what we hear and expect to hear from our organizations to indicate we are delivering the outcomes they expect. Our organizations say:

Because of the ZL framework ...
- *We have grown faster.*

- *We are more profitable.*

- *We work together better.*
    - *Know what is expected in all directions*
    - *Get encouraged often*
    - *Empowered and not abandoned*
    - *Engaged with all parts*
    - *More included in decision-making*
    - *Better use of other management tools*
    - *More effective and efficient*
- *We have more clarity, focus, and simplicity.*

- *There is less stress, chaos, and dysfunction.*

- *We apply new things more effectively.*

- *Individual engagement is increased.*

- *Innovation and ongoing refinement is now easier.*

(2) Consultants, Coaches, Mentors (Certified Coaches):

Following is what we hear and expect to hear from our Certified Coaches to indicate we are delivering what they expect. Our Certified Coaches say:

*Because of the **ZL** framework ...*
- *Our clients are more successful.*

- *We are more successful.*

- *We are more deeply engaged with clients.*
    - *Know what is going on at all times*
    - *Know what is expected in all directions*
    - *Get recognized explicitly for input*
    - *Active with all parts of the organization*
    - *Included at all times in decision-making*
    - *Orchestrate other coaching specialists*
    - *More effective and efficient*
    - *An essential part of leading and managing*

- *We create more clarity, focus, and simplicity.*

- *There is less stress, chaos, and dysfunction.*

- *We apply what is learned more effectively.*

- *Innovation and ongoing refinement is now easier.*

- *We have a virtual and ubiquitous presence.*

All the above needs to be edited and updated from time to time. Our commitment is to exceptional performance. We've coined a new phrase to help motivate us with a bit of humor included. The code for our phrase is OCE™. OCD is used as a code for Obsessive Compulsive Disorder. Our OCE™ stands for Obsessive Compulsive Excellence™. Attention to detail with a commitment to excellence is a part of each one of us. We think this exists in great measure in all great organizations.

We use OCE™ jokingly and we use it seriously. We use it frequently lest we forget. The need for innovation and excellence are fun and never-ending dimensions to life. Adding humor to very serious issues adds value and relief.

Striving for excellence is different than being consumed by it. Excellence is not perfection. Striving is illustrated by an ongoing operating commitment, not achieving perfection. When mistakes/failures occur it's important to give the mistake/failure its fair/perfunctory nod, fix it, and then move on. Yes, acknowledge it, but don't continue thinking about it. Assume the right lessons have been learned and dwell on the positives of the new learning.

Summary

Whom we serve and *how* we serve them is paramount. Being thankful for those you serve and proud of how you do it is foundational to the well-being of an organization. The more intensely, broadly, and profoundly the individuals in an organization believe and live up to this

45

expectation of themselves, the greater will be their performance and impact individually and collectively.

The more carefully you define and focus who you can and should serve, the more successful you will be. The examples given in this chapter should help you refine your descriptions. Documenting your thinking and making it available to others is a great first step. Including others in this process and reviewing regularly to make sure you're both on track and adjusting, as needed, is necessary to stay on your path of continuous improvement.

Excellence is not perfection. Excellence is attained by doing everything extremely well and still acknowledging mistakes/failures, fixing them, learning from them, and then moving on with a new sense of accomplishment.

Every company has two organizational structures: The formal one is written on the charts; the other is the everyday relationship of the men and women in the organization.

—Harold S. Geneen

4. Our Organization

How we work together as a team

The organization chart is the layout of the various parts and dimensions of the working community. Traditionally it's drawn to show hierarchy in terms of who reports to whom. It's also a diagram to establish territories in terms of who is in charge of what. There is a tendency for this type of chart to encourage others to see the organization solely in terms of its individual contributors.

I'm proposing an addition and alternative. It helps if individuals also understand what and how their organization's parts are supposed to create value for its customers. This establishes the premise that the parts working together to serve the customers is a first-level focus. This minimizes a common development in which leaders of different parts evolve to the state where they feel they are responsible mostly for protecting their part (territory) from everything including the other parts of the same organization.

a. Chart

Following is a skeletal version of our functional organization chart. It presents the primary departments designed to make the organization work effectively. Their primary focus and area of contribution are contained in their title.

Zynity, LLC
Functional Organization Diagram

| Marketing | Sales | Training | Support | Operations | Website | Fin/Acctg |

The chart on the preceding page presents the functional departments within our organization. This is the most traditional style of presenting the departments within an organization—the formal structure. Our Zynity Leadership tools and the methodology are used to keep the leaders of each department connected and aligned. The departments also use the tools to connect and align the leading and managing team within each department.

A second chart will be presented in the following pages, which add more explanation for each of the departments. The exercise in creating this second one is to add a conceptual perspective with details to aid understanding. This chart defines how the individuals in the organization are expected to work in their everyday relationships.

Notice in the second chart, in the column added to the left are the titles for the information listed under each department. The departments are referred to as **components**. This is a term that becomes more meaningful as we expand on how we are customer focused. Each department is a component of the customer's experience. Also, each department has a clearly defined set of **customers**. The **theme** for each department is one word describing its primary role. Each department has something to **deliver** that benefits the entire organization. There is a specific type of **technology**(ies) used by each department to help it conduct its activities more effectively.

In the following chart is listed, for each department, who they serve, what they do, what they deliver, and the technology used to improve their activities. As this is a new way of presenting an organization you will read the explanation after the chart repeats this again in a different style (more detail) to help as many understand as possible.

Probably obvious, but may go unnoticed, is there are no names of individuals. Often organizations get defined by the talents and presence of individuals and never grow out of it. This effort of defining by operational needs and contributions is essential if an organization is to grow beyond the capabilities of individuals.

Individuals are important. Individuals in the early days of an organization often make enormously important contributions to its growth. Documenting the organization in this way makes it easier to understand the needs of the organization so roles can be migrated to meet the real needs and not just accommodate the talents of individuals.

Growing organizations are always changing. The perspective provided by this type of chart allows an organization to adopt and adapt to new things more readily and easily. As the organization is being defined and understood in this way we must also consider the individual.

Individuals are essential to the evolving of an organization. They must be changing as well. Everyone must have their own professional and personal development plan outlined and defined. (There is a place for this in our online tools.) The better we define and evolve the organization, the easier it is for individuals to define and evolve their own development plans.

Zynity, LLC
Operational Organization Diagram

Components:	Marketing	Sales	Training	Support	Operations	Website	Fin/Acctg
Customer Categories:	Subscribers Coaches Alliances Vendors	Subscribers Coaches Alliances Channels	Subscribers Coaches Alliances Vendors	Subscribers Coaches Alliances Vendors	Subscribers Coaches Internal Staff	Subscribers Coaches Alliances Vendors	Subscribers Coaches Alliances Vendors
Theme/Role:	Attract	Acquire	Engage	Nurture	Capabilities	Infrastructure	Monitor
Deliverables:	Leads Market Definitions Ideas	Closes Ideas	Onboarding Expanding Ideas	Usage Migration Ideas	Staff Reports Productivity	Visits Education Attraction	# Reports $ Reports Cash
Basic Tech:	SFA, Email	SFA	OnLine Ed, CRM	CRM	ETW	Hosting	Acctg/CRM

Outside Professionals:
Legal, Finance, HR, Training, Processes, Technology, Marketing, Contact Centers

Following is a more detailed explanation of the parts. This detailed explanation may seem tedious to some, but it helps significantly to belabor the descriptions, so everyone can better grasp the conceptual understandings of the parts of the organization.

The chart/diagram included on the preceding page is for our online SaaS business model. The component headings could be slightly different for a manufacturing or consulting organization. In our chart the columns are the functional parts, and rows are the following: [Each row is a title for the content and focus in each functional part (column). For example, the row titled Deliver contains the tangible contributions made by each functional part.]

- Component
- Customer categories
- Theme/role
- Deliver
- Basic tech

Components is used to designate and clarify the functional parts of all the chart from Marketing to Finance and Accounting. The term *component* is used to designate it as a "part" of the whole needed to serve customers completely. Spectacular customer experiences are accomplished when all parts (components) do their activities spectacularly.

Customer categories include the external customers as well as the internal customers served by each functional part.

Theme/role is the focus and contribution of each functional part.

Deliverables are the tangible and measurable items each functional part creates with/for their customers in the organization.

Basic tech is the type of technology each component uses to enhance their productivity.

Each functional part is diagrammed in terms of who it serves, what it creates, and the technology it uses to make all they do happen effectively. Obviously, but worth noting, the parts are presented left to right in the flow of the sequence in which the organization connects with its customers. This is the beginning of understanding how customers perceive the organization works from their viewpoint.

b. Character, culture, and core values

Our **character** is dominated by the strong personalities and competitiveness of the professionals who are employee as well as non-employee resources. Non-employee resources include our network of certified coaches and the employees of our much-respected professional resources.

* * *
Each individual must be treated as if they're first.
* * *

The customer is first focus. Professionals may perceive their position as first as they're necessary to create the right experience for each customer every time. The idea of first shouldn't be defined by *either/or* but rather *and*. Our professionals and customers are of equal value and importance as they're individuals. There doesn't have to be a trade-off or play one against the other to satisfy and serve both.

Customers are not always right in their demands or manner of engaging with us. We engage to achieve right thinking and feeling with them in all instances. We bend to meet their demands and leave room for the reality that we can't please everyone all the time.

Our **culture** evolves (becomes more effective) around the need for each professional to excel at what they do. Individuals want to clearly know what is expected of them. They need to be equipped and prepared to do all they're supposed to do.

* * *
Expectations are clear and expected.
* * *

Individuals and teams expect to be recognized for their exceptional performance. They desire to execute and innovate in high-performing ways as they collaborate with their peers (and all individuals are their peers). In some roles and situations individuals are subordinate to others and submit accordingly. It's done in an attitude of mutual respect as styles and personal preferences are honored.

* * *

Lore and core values

* * *

How we talk about ourselves within our organization and to those outside establishes our identity. The organization is characterized by the sum of its stories. The **stories** are a key part of building and shaping our culture. The accumulation of our stories makes up our lore. Each story is part of the bigger story. Our events and how we share them with others is critical to developing our culture.

Our **core values** are the foundations upon which we're building our character and culture. They are best expressed in the following sound bites:

Individuals are most important – In all we do we consider its impact on individuals. It begins with the person next to us and continues with all those with whom we connect.

Do the big things – We must always see the big picture keeping each event in perspective. Concepts, principles, past, present, and future are important considerations in all things.

Do the small things – Results of all kinds are distinguished by how well the details are accomplished. Opportunities and successes are in the details.

Integrity in all things – There are no substitutes or alternatives for openness and honesty.

Deliver on all promises – Meeting commitments always and exceeding expectations as often as possible separates individuals and organizations from their peers.

Innovate continuously – Begin with the frankness that change isn't always fun. Continue the processes of changing as needed with the motive that almost all things can and should be improved.

c. Working together – ZL Managing Team Suite

ZL is an abbreviation for Zynity Leadership™. The **Managing Team Suite** is a set of online tools found at www.Zynity.com. This suite is used to connect and align the deliverables and activities of everyone on the leading and managing team. This is where we share each individual's **top issues** for the coming week and communicate to keep one another in the loop about our individual and mutual issues daily. The sharing is done within defined teams so only those with need will know.

As you know, website development is a constant process of updates. Rather than show you a screen shot of this tool, it's preferable for you to go to the website www.Zynity.com and see it in its current form and style.

The **top issues** are first shared as a brief title or description which we call a **headline**. Each headline communicates a single top issue. After the headline is established you can add more information about the headline, which is the **story**. The headline is a short label to help others determine if they want to read more of the story that goes along with the headline.

* * *

Headlines and stories

* * *

The headline is all that's shown when opening the sharing tool to keep the amount of information brief. If someone wants to read more, they click the icon to expand the headline for the rest of the story. The content placed in this suite of tools is for sharing the top issues facing each one on the team. This includes their current activities and the things they're planning to accomplish in the coming week.

A weekly schedule of updating and starting a new set of headlines keeps everyone current and in the loop. Each person on the team can make comments and add messages to everyone else's headlines. This is a way for others to add input and insights as well as encouragement and celebrations about specific headlines. It's a way to give feedback and send/receive messages while staying on point as guided by the headline. It builds a form of C-level speaking, forcing each one to stay brief and on topic. All issues are shared in headline and story format throughout all the tools.

You can also attach a document or include a link as part of a headline's story to add more relevance and support to the story. Again, when it is displayed it is a brief headline and the reader clicks to get the rest of the story. This reduces the amount of reading required to get to the meat of top issues. Each can easily engage or ignore as they choose. These various exchanges are in the headline tool between selected parties in a team. Teams are formed by Team Facilitators and are usually comprised of a department or group such as top-level management, a functional area leading and managing team, or the principal with a board of directors.

The top issues being shared as headlines and related stories is the same with all tools in each of the suites. In the following chapters, we'll use the term headline to identify this as a single element of communicating. The leading and managing of organizations requires simple, clear, and focused communicating. Headlines are the fundamental feature and building blocks in all the ZL suites of tools. They facilitate the need to communicate succinctly. They also facilitate the need to communicate broadly within teams without inundating each one with too much information. Each team quickly evolves its guidelines to ensure exchanges are pointed and succinct.

* * *

Deliverables and Activities

* * *

The primary tool in this Managing Team suite is the DnAs™. This is an acronym representing **Deliverables**

and Activities. Each deliverable and each activity are shared as a headline. There are different Weekly DnAs™ for each person in the organization. Sharing these with selected individuals in a disciplined and scheduled manner enhances communicating and collaborating throughout the week. Getting top-level-issues information in a digital form and sharing across our devices creates new ways of collaborating and thinking.

There are different Role DnAs™ for each person in the organization. Defining one's role in terms of their deliverables and activities helps them and others know the contributions expected of them. Deliverables are tangible outputs such as sales or a report. Activities take time to accomplish (such as a meeting) and support deliverability but don't directly create a tangible output.

The objective in this chapter is to share the various types of content (information) to place in this suite of tools. Use of the tools is as simple as using email. It's easy and quick to get others working and sharing in the tools. There is significant emphasis about determining which content to include in the tools.

As a group, we learn how to use the content better after it's in the tools. It's a collaboration tool with guidance on what content to share and how to share it. Again, the content shared in this suite of tools is for sharing the top issues facing each one, the things they are doing, and the things they are planning to do in the coming week.

The fifth book in the *A Framework for Leading*™ series presents a more complete explanation about using the methodology and online tools to enhance communicating and performance of the leading and managing team. The subtitle of this fifth book is *Connect and Align*. Its theme is "Communicating in High-Performance Organizations."

* * *

Connect and align the team.

* * *

Experience shows that achieving effective and efficient communication while going at warp speed is an ongoing challenge. These tools are proven to overcome that challenge.

Collaborative online tools may be new for some. They're not new for those already using project management tools or CRM (Customer Relationship Management) or SFA (Sales Force Automation) tools online. Even in these organizations, there was a time when their organization's content was only available in a more manual or lower-level digital tool. Having the content available in these browser-based specifically designed functionally focused leading and managing tools make the content much more usable and impactful. The result: better information and better collaboration.

* * *

Make information accessible and useful.

* * *

Quality of decisions improve, and productivity increases significantly as information is more accessible and usable with these online tools. It's a part of the benefit of the normal migration of using more technology. This also makes the work environment more vibrant and reduces stress. The right content used correctly engages talented individuals.

Summary

How the team works together is as important as how they work individually. The diagram of how the parts are designed to work together is just an outline. Each part has its role to serve. The individuals and the environment in which they work determine the performance of the individuals and the organization.

The lore of an organization describes who and what it is. The stories shared about the organization shape its culture. They establish a persona for those within the organization and those outside the organization.

The core values are the most important ingredients in determining the organization's culture and character. The more explicitly character, culture, and core values are defined and adhered to, the more likely the individuals and the organization will be who they say they want to be.

It is not enough to be busy;
so are the ants.
The question is:
what are we busy about?

—Henry David Thoreau

5. New Ways and New Things

Making new things happen

Choosing what each one should be doing in advance is more productive than everyone simply reacting to the urgent needs of the moment. Yes, there are the basic everyday needs of the business that are constant, frequent, and essential. Some roles are specifically designed to accommodate these everyday needs as their full-time focus. These should be considered in the disciplines we will present below. However, there's also a need for deliberate budgeting of time and resources to allow for new things and continually improving the constant, frequent, and essential things.

It seems to be easier to repeatedly do time-consuming workarounds (coping) than creating and executing new ways (solving). Why is it difficult to do things in new ways and new things?

(1) Thinking ahead requires deliberate focus.
(2) Getting busy removes the urge/desire for new things.
(3) How to execute new things takes thinking and changing.
(4) Seldom can you be certain new things will accomplish all you hope.

... add to this list as you wish.

Be encouraged by this thought; great leaps of improvement are made over time with small, refining steps. Be deliberate. Be focused. Be unrelenting.

An organization's capability to innovate and do new things is the single most important ingredient for it to survive and thrive for a long period. Doing very well what you did yesterday is essential. Doing new things just as well is necessary for Surthrival™. *Surthrival*™ is our new noun combining the two verbs *surviving* and *thriving* to describe the condition of a vibrant organization. Ergo, the new compliment is that the organization is in an enviable state of Surthrival™.

a. Opportunities and innovation

A key part of leadership is preparing for innovating and new opportunities. Opportunities include new products to sell or another organization to buy. Innovation can be a new way of doing something you already do or creating a new product or service to sell.

Getting new opportunities and innovations to become a part of the constant, frequent, and essential, requires they be implemented into the existing organizational activities. This can be complicated to accomplish. This complication barrier is one of the more common limitations impacting the growth and well-being of organizations. The ideas are there, and the value is clear. The steps for implementing are not so clear. The needs of constant, frequent, and essential keep moving the dates for planning and implementation of the new.

It takes structure, process, and discipline to make the complexity of doing new things manageable. It begins with assessing the value of an idea. If an idea is deemed to have merit and creates value, then we establish a strategic initiative to make the idea a reality. We follow the steps outlined in the following section of this chapter to get it implemented.

Ideas + Strategic Initiatives + Implementation = Value Creation

There are many great books, seminars, and consultants that have great teachings about strategies. We are not teaching strategies here. We are focused on providing guidance and a tool to help implement your strategic ideas. We recommend consulting experts and facilitators as needed for strategy sessions. Once the strategies are established, the following information about strategic initiatives will help get them prioritized and implemented.

b. Strategic Initiatives – ZL Strategies Suite

Strategies are needed to create and implement new things. They begin with an idea that encompasses why it's needed and being done. The term strategy is used to encompass both a *what to do* and a *how to do it*. It's usually something to establish an advantage in the organization's operations or sales growth. These are needed when an organization is committed to growth and willing to do new things. Clarifying strategies and carefully planning initiatives is essential for them to succeed.

A **strategic initiative** (*what* and *how*) is a commitment with a set of steps to get the strategy implemented. A complex strategy may require a set of related initiatives to get it implemented.

* * *

They can be simple or complex.

* * *

Some strategic initiatives (SI) can be relatively simple and others very complex. Simple strategies usually require that an incremental new thing be accomplished. Updating a technology tool currently in use can be relatively simple and requires only incremental changes to get it implemented.

* * *

Leap – Reach – Stretch™ initiatives

* * *

Strategic initiatives can be very complex. I call these **Leap – Reach – Stretch**™ initiatives. These are things the organization has either not done before or not done at the new planned scale. Examples are an acquisition or adding new channels to double sales in two years.

It's possible to execute a strategic initiative at the wrong time. It's even more common to execute one without proper planning. It is also possible to get too many strategic initiatives underway without the needed focus and resources.

* * *

Prioritize and schedule initiatives.

* * *

We begin the exploration of possible strategic initiatives with an Initiative Worksheet™ (IW). The purpose of the worksheet is to define the initiative. This is completed at the very outset of an idea. This Initiative Worksheet™ is one of the tools in the ZL Strategies Suite.

As you know, website development is a constant process of updates. Rather than show you a screen shot of this tool, it's preferable for you to go to the website <u>www.Zynity.com</u> and see it in its current form and style.

* * *

Consider this business rule.

* * *

The business rule in our organization is that the owner of the idea must take time to complete this worksheet before they discuss it with another person. After they have it in a first draft but acceptable shape, they can discuss it with one other person. If the other person thinks it's a good idea, and will date and initial the worksheet, then the idea can be discussed with others. These others are those who can help assess its value and contributions to the organization.

* * *

Don't let new ideas be a distraction.

* * *

This early preparation process is helpful in organizations where there is someone with lots of ideas that take up others' time with ideas not fully developed. This can be a great distraction. In organizations where there isn't one or more persons with lots of ideas, it still helps the assessment of possible ideas get accomplished with more discipline. The categories in the worksheet are as follows:

- Owner
- Date
- Initiative Name
- Description
- Purpose
- Hard Measurables
- Soft Measurables
- Resources
- Barriers, Risks, Downsides
- Implementation schedule
- Supporter

Owner is the individual with the idea. This may be one or more individuals.

Date is the day on which this form is started with the specific idea. It's ok to note the date when you're thinking about this first started in the notes section.

Initiative Name is the title (one or very few words) labeling the idea.

Description is an explanation of the idea in one or a few sentences.

Purpose is an explanation of why it should be done and what it should accomplish.

Hard Measurables are the items or results that can be expressed in numbers.

Soft Measurables are the benefit items that can be expressed in feelings, attitudes, or motives.

Resources are the ingredients required to make it happen.

Barriers, Risk, Downsides are the negatives to consider in assessing the value and likelihood of success and possible value creation.

Implementation Schedule is the possible and likely best time to start and work the initiative. The length of implementation is as important as the start date. Spreading a strategic initiative out over time can help allocate better use of scarce resources or doing it quickly can create more value sooner.

Supporter is the other individual(s) (not the idea owner) who are presented with this idea for the first time after this form is in first draft status. This is affirmation others need to be engaged for next steps.

As a reminder, we've labeled this section with the pullout of don't let new ideas be a distraction. Often ideas get shared broadly before thought-through and build hopes or frustrations unnecessarily because the idea never sees the light of day. This step with the Initiative Worksheet™ (IW) is intended to reduce this phenomenon. Only thought-through ideas should be shared broadly and even then, with caution.

It is important to schedule when approved initiatives can begin. Organizations may have more than one initiative to get underway. They need to be tracked. Each initiative has a life of its own. There are participants and spectators for each initiative. Keeping everyone in the loop and engaged in their role will be a challenge at times.

* * *

Keeping everyone engaged with initiatives.

* * *

Prioritizing the sequence of when a strategic initiative is ready and should be started is an important set of decisions for the leading and managing team. There may be many initiatives started and underway at the same time in various parts of the organization. The following paragraph introduces a suite of tools to facilitate leading and managing multiple initiatives.

Sequencing initiatives should consider where the most immediate value can be created, and which one needs to be finished first to maximize the value potential for others. It's possible it may be necessary to put one already underway on pause while a new idea (initiative) gets completed. They are often intertwined in their potential and impact.

The **ZL Strategies Suite** is a set of online tools located at the website www.Zynity.com (ZL is an abbreviation for Zynity Leadership™). We use this suite to keep track of all the various strategic initiatives underway in our organization. This is where we communicate with headlines (refer to chapter 3 for more information about the meaning and use of headlines) to keep one another in the loop about our individual and mutual issues with the ongoing initiatives.

Examples of this suite of tools are available at the website. The content shared in this suite of tools is for sharing the top issues required to define and complete strategic initiatives to grow the organization, add new capabilities, and revamp or update existing capabilities. All issues are shared in headline and story format throughout the tools.

> **As you know, website development is a constant process of updates. Rather than show you a screen shot of this tool, it's preferable for you to go to the website www.Zynity.com and see it in its current form and style.**

Another tool in this suite is the SIPs™. This is an acronym representing the name **Strategic Initiative Plans™**. There can be different active SIPs™ for different parts of the organization.

The objective in this chapter is to share the various types of content to place in this suite of tools. Use of the tools is as simple as using email. We easily and quickly get others working and sharing in the tools. There is a bit of learning about which content to include in the tools. As a group, we learn how to use the content better after it's in the tools. It's a collaboration tool with guidance on what content to share and how to share it.

Each strategic initiative is listed in a headline form in the tool with its projected completion dates. There are communications each week (and daily if needed) within the tool to update everyone with progress and invites. Everyone makes comments and suggestions whether they're an active participant or a concerned spectator. This ongoing input and interaction helps. It's better to keep everyone informed as we go along rather than waiting for meetings later. The quality of the input is often better when it's shared as the thinking occurs rather than making notes and sharing later. The sharing is done in a manner to allow each one to read and respond on their own schedule without risk of being out of the loop.

Various teams (management team, departments, special groups) defined by team facilitators create their own list of initiatives for their team. This keeps each one on the team connected with the activities and progress of each initiative. Each person is kept in the loop and can easily add their ideas and comments as the initiatives are formed and implemented. It can get a bit complicated when an idea impacts two areas in positive and challenging ways. This requires even more planning and preparation to get it accomplished correctly.

The sixth book in the *A Framework for Leading*™ series presents a more complete explanation of using the methodology and its suite of online tools to enhance developing and implementing strategies. The subtitle of this sixth book is *Strategic Initiatives*. Its theme is "Creating, Prioritizing, and Implementing Strategies."

Summary

Discipline creating, prioritizing, and implementing strategic initiatives is essential for growing an organization. Keeping all relevant parties informed and focused without hours of meetings can be done with the ZL Strategies Suite of online tools.

This is a high-level approach to keeping participants and spectators engaged on an as-we-go basis without getting them buried in the details. The details are handled by the implementers who may in some cases use an online project management tool to help the implementation team stay on track with the details.

A business is simply an idea to make other individuals' lives better.

—Richard Branson

6. Being Customer Focused

Always see the customer's view.

Most organizations say they are customer focused. Not many have a document, or set of documents, clearly expressing and measuring how each part of the organization is customer focused. Over time it's so easy for organizations to become inwardly focused. We are always fixing and changing how we do things internally. How these internal fixes impact the customer is often minimized or ignored completely.

The following presents our written explanation of how we're customer focused. It's used and understood by each employee within a few days of starting with the organization. Their understanding and agreement is assessed as a part of their introductory orientation.

a. Categories

We have the following categories of customers and clients. Each one represents a unique set of entities with distinct and shared needs.

- Individuals
- Organizations subscribing to our tools
- Users within the subscribing organizations
- Certified Coaches
- Our employees
- Vendors
- Professional resources

Each category connects with the organization in a different way and with different expectations. Clarifying their expectations guides and structures our connection to maximize the desired benefit. One of our business rules is to understand the value we bring to each category of customer or client. We get them to verify the specifics. We establish measurements to guide us in meeting those specific expectations.

* * *

Categories are viewed as distinct.

* * *

The seventh book in the *A Framework for Leading*™ series presents a more complete explanation of using the methodology and this suite of online tools to enhance attracting, engaging, and serving each category of customer. The subtitle of this seventh book is *Customers and Clients*. Its theme is "Structure to Attract, Engage, and Serve."

Change is a part of life. We deliberately review how well we're doing for *Customers and Clients* each month along with our daily interactions. We make the needed adjustments to continue improving all we do.

b. Customer's view – ZL Customer's Suite

The **ZL Customer's Suite** is a set of online tools located at the website www.Zynity.com. (ZL is an abbreviation for Zynity Leadership™.) I use this suite to keep track of all the various details about the categories of customers. It's here where we communicate to keep one another in the loop about our individual and mutual issues with all the various customers. Demos of this suite of tools are available at the website. The content shared in this suite of tools is for sharing the top issues required to attract, engage, and serve customers and clients. All issues are shared in headline and story format throughout the tools.

As you know, website development is a constant process of updates. Rather than show you a screen shot of this tool, it's preferable for you to go to the website www.Zynity.com and see it in its current form and style.

The primary tool in this suite is the C-Vyoos™. This is an acronym representing the name **Customer's View of your organization's operations**. Each category of customer is developed in its own C-Vyoos™. The page developed for each category is a matrix with rows and columns.

The objective of this chapter is to share the various types of content to place in this suite of tools. Use of the tools is as simple as using email. All sharing of top issues is done with a headline and its related story. We can easily and quickly get others working and sharing in the tools with us. It's easy to learn which content to include in the tools. As a group, we learn how to use the content better after it's in the tools. It is a collaboration tool with guidance on what content to share and how to share it.

Columns for the matrix

The column headings are usually different for each category (type) of customer and client. Column headings for our second category, **organizations**, are as follows:

- Awareness
- Connect
- Share
- Committed
- Schedule
- Training
- Support
- Add-on training
- Migration
- Ongoing success

Awareness is about getting the right prospects to be aware of us and for us to become aware of them.

Connect is about getting them in our pipeline with their contact information so we can arrange a call or meeting.

Share is what gets accomplished in the phone call, chat, seminar, webinar, or face-to-face meeting. They share their needs and understanding. We share, what we have, to help them.

Committed is the condition of both parties as the organization decides to implement the methodology and online tools.

Schedule are the dates and times established for the parties in both organizations to work together.

Training are the classes, webinars, tutorials, and online courses individuals will take for implementation.

Support is the availability of ZL trainers and Certified Coaches to help individuals in the early stages of getting started.

Add-on training is the classes, webinars, tutorials, and online courses individuals take to use the advanced tools in a suite or start using the basic tools in another suite.

Migration is a set of processes that help organizations assess the value of the tools and determine how they help in their growth. It's a time of refining how the tools are used and how their impact will be measured.

Ongoing success is the stage where ZL and organizations determine how all this impacts their growth trajectory and longevity. Organizations should have a strong sense of thriving and how their strength now impacts their customers and clients.

The row headings are the same for all categories. It's important to remember each category is comprised of individuals. It's the experiences for each individual we seek to clarify and understand in this tool.

* * *

Rows for the matrix

* * *

The headings for each row are fixed as follows:
- Stages
- Results
- Activities
- Contributors
- Helpers
- Reports

Stages identify the various evolving steps to attract, engage, and nurture the relationship with the individuals in each category.

Results are the deliverables to be created in each stage.

Activities are the many things done in each stage to create the results.

Contributors are the individuals or groups providing activities and input in the stage.

Helpers are the things needed to enable the activities and results in the stage.

Reports contain the items to be measured to ensure the stage is creating its intended results in a manner benefitting the organization.

The above descriptions highlight the definitions of the rows. These are fixed for all users.

The columns may be changed for each category within each organization. You will edit the columns to suit your organization and its categories. Gathering the headlines for each component of the matrix only takes about an hour with the right coaching and facilitating. The information already exists in your organization. You just need to take the time and thought to express it in the tools in headline and story form. Once the basics are in the tool, you'll add to it very easily, as needed, over time. It's like organizing a garage or warehouse. Once the sections are marked off, it's easy to put things in their places. Once in their places, they are far more accessible and usable.

Summary

Customer focus requires more than saying we care about our customers and how we perform our work. Just saying something doesn't make it true. Great success is dependent on implementing the details in exceptional fashion.

Getting the customer focused information organized in an accessible place makes it far more usable. It's also easier for others in the organization to understand consistently and work together seamlessly.

The matrix created with the C-Vyoos™ tool is a way to structure your organization around how it attracts, engages, and nurtures customers. A strong case can be made for organizing around how you serve customers and clients. This is being customer focused. Being able to show customers and clients the structure on a laptop is an even stronger statement. Having everyone in your organization understand and use the tool is the final convicting and convincing event to understand its value.

*If a measurement matters at all,
it is because it must have
some conceivable effect
on decisions and behaviour.*

—Douglas W. Hubbard

7. Eyes on the Numbers

Deliberate attention pays great rewards.

Everyone seems to agree it's very important to put reporting in place to measure results. Without some type of measuring and frequent reviewing, the results may not be as desired. Numbers are also needed to stimulate, focus, and guide growth.

It begins with budgets. Budgets express expectations. If expectations aren't met or exceeded (the reports let us know), we need to assess our expectations or adjust the activities being used to create the results.

Being extra deliberate and attentive to results and how we measure them has a big impact on the predictability and quality of expected results. Establishing the right measurements is foundational to leading and managing an organization.

Leading is marked by doing right things while considering their impact on the future. Managing is marked by doing things right in the present. Much of a leader's role is managing. Some of a manager's role is leading. Both require the proper use of measurements.

* * *

Use these accounting reports properly.

* * *

At a minimum, there are three basic financial reports: **profit and loss**, **cash flow**, and **balance sheet**. Our surveys suggest there is vastly less attention to these than is needed. Not understanding their usefulness and how to glean important information from them is the usual explanation for why they're often given little or casual attention. Sustainable success starts with using these three reports frequently and properly. Each one provides a specific and necessary perspective about the financial condition of the organization.

Following is a simple explanation of what they present when correctly prepared and used.

Profit and loss
This report calculates profit or loss by subtracting expenses from revenues. If losses persist, the organization will likely cease operations. If profits are small, the organization will likely not grow. If profits are strong, the organization can grow and thrive. Individuals like to work for thriving organizations as it's usually more fun. The most basic structure of this report is:

$$\textbf{Revenue} - \textbf{expenses} = \textbf{profit}$$

The next most basic structure of this report is:

$100 Revenue
-60 – Cost of goods
40 = Gross margin
-30 – Administrative costs
$10 = Profit

The **most basic** lets us know if we're making a profit at all. The **next most basic** lets us know if we're making enough margin when we sell an item. (Sell for $100 and buy for $60 = a $40 gross margin. If there is no gross margin you're deeply in trouble.) Once we know we have a good gross margin then we can turn our attention to making sure we properly manage our administrative expenses. Each level of detail gives additional insights about the organization.

Decisions impacted by this report have to do with generating sales and managing costs. It's the first indicator used to identify which part of the organization needs the most and/or immediate attention.

Cash flow

This report calculates cash created by subtracting cash going out from cash coming in. If cash created is zero or less, the organization may likely have ceased operations sometime prior. If it's only slightly positive, growth will be stunted. If cash created is strongly positive, the organization can thrive. The saying "cash is king" refers to the importance of cash and it needs to be accounted for and understood very well. Following is the most basic structure of this report.

Cash in (minus) Cash out = Cash created

The next most basic structure of this report is as follows:

Cash in	
Receivables/sales	**$100**
Loans	**0**
Total cash in	**$100**
Cash out	
Bills	**$ 50**
Payroll	**35**
Total cash out	**$ 85**
= Cash created	**$ 15**

Decisions impacted by this report are about proper billing and prompt collection of receivables. You pay bills with cash or loans or credit cards (another type of loan).

Balance sheet

This report calculates the net worth of the organization by subtracting liabilities from assets. If a negative net worth persists, the organization will likely cease operations. If it's only slightly positive, growth will be stunted. If net worth is strongly positive, the organization might thrive.

This report is a summary of the combined impact of the activities from the profit and loss and the cash flow statements. Banks and investors use this report to give them an understanding of the current and trending financial health of the organization at the end of an operating period, say a month, quarter, or year. This report should be created and used monthly. It's a bit more complicated but in its simplest form it looks like this:

Assets = liabilities + net worth

In its next simplest form, it looks like this:

Assets (things we own)
$100   Cash
$400   Other
$500   Total assets (all we own)

Liabilities (things we owe)
$100   Bills
$200   Loans
$300   Total liabilities (all we owe)

Net worth (Owed to Owners)
$200   Earnings (profits in the company)
$200   Total net worth (Owner's Equity)

$500   Total liabilities + net worth

Assets always equal total liabilities plus net worth. This truth is one indication accountants can know they've done all the other accounting transactions properly. Don't ask them why about this unless you're prepared to take and do well in a few accounting classes. Please imagine a smiley emoji here.

Consider these two circumstances:

> One organization has $100 in assets, $50 in liabilities, and $50 in net worth. It's deemed healthy. If this one used its assets to pay its liabilities, it would have $50 remaining.

> Another organization has $100 in assets, $150 in liabilities, and –$50 in net worth. It's deemed very unhealthy. If this one used all its assets to pay its liabilities, it would still owe $50 more.

> Decisions impacted by this report are about what to do with capital needs, capital options, and the ability of the organization to obtain additional capital.

These reports are not simple to create correctly. Nor are they easy to understand without training. Developing and using them well is an essential capability for building a thriving organization. Remember this: accountants prepare the reports and leaders and managers use the reports. Leaders and managers don't need to become accountants, but they do have to become very good at using the reports. So, don't worry about how they get created. Learn how to use the information they provide.

Creating them using proper accounting principles takes a lot of training. There is also some art in developing the presentation of the properly developed details (what gets presented and how) so they are helpful to your organization. This requires deliberate and detailed collaboration between accounting and leadership.

Sharing, at first, isn't always easy but the outcomes are worth the effort.

There are organizations who use these reports properly. There are organizations who don't. If you don't, we suggest you do so and quickly. It'll help you measure and manage your operations more efficiently and effectively. You'll make faster and better decisions about strategic issues and opportunities. You'll increase your likelihood of building a thriving organization.

The eighth book in the *A Framework for Leading* ™ series presents a more complete explanation of using the reporting methodology and this suite of online tools to guide the activities in each part of the organization. The subtitle of this eighth book is *Measurements*. Its theme is "Measuring and Managing the Right Things."

This is intended to highlight the need for integrating the roles of accounting and reporting with the other leading and managing teams within the organization. Almost every activity in an organization can be quantified. If it can be quantified, it should be. If quantified, it should be viewed and used in making decisions.

* * *

Rely on accountants for accounting, but ...

* * *

You don't have to understand how these reports are created by the accounting individuals. You do have to be able to understand them or rely on others who do. This includes asking them questions about sections of the reports to get input for the decisions you need to make. This makes it easier to determine what you need to do differently. Getting very good at this doesn't take a lot of time. It'll be one of the best investments of your time and all other leaders and managers in your organization. If you can't understand the scoring very well, it is likely you won't play so well.

a. Budgets, benchmarks, and forecasting

The monthly performance and budget review is an essential meeting. It's here the learning and growing continues. It's here we know if we're making progress. It can't be done without a budget.

Budgeting is the process of putting expected numbers in categories for future time periods in a spreadsheet or in an accounting system. An example is the revenues expected each month for the coming year. It also includes putting the numbers in place for the expected expenses required to create those revenues in the same time periods. The difference between revenues and the expenses is important. This difference is the *margin* in non-profits and the *profit* in for-profit organizations. Both types of entities need to know their margins or profits.

The value of creating and using a budget is manifold. It forces thinking about the future. It causes individuals to make commitments. It identifies areas needing to be done in new ways. It identifies new opportunities. It helps establish priorities. It leads to specific plans and makes way for much more. Without a budget, budgeting process, and disciplined budget reviews with actuals, it's easier to repeat past errors and not learn from current experiences.

* * *

Budgeting is for dreamers.

* * *

Budgeting is a time for expanding one's views and perspective. It's a time for challenging. It's a time for setting direction. It's a time for setting boundaries. It's a time for moving boundaries. It's a time for reflection and assessment. It's a time for motivating. It's a time for being more of who you want to be. It's the way to begin understanding the costs and resources required to create specific current and new revenue sources. The numbers help you understand what to do and how to do the selected path more effectively.

An organization without a budget and a budgeting process may do some of the things above, but they'll likely be significantly less successful in their accomplishments. Their competitors who do budgeting will continue to outperform them at most or all levels.

* * *

Budgeting helps everyone.

* * *

Budgeting should be embraced by more than just the accounting types. Leaders and managers should also be capable of creating and understanding a budget and the budgeting process. It may be necessary to get help with the budgeting process. It will be time and money well

93

spent. The better the budget, the better the organization performs. Each unit gets their goals from the budget.

By the way, after the budget is ready, using it becomes its own great reward. Using the monthly financial budgets and other operating results to compare with the related budgets opens doors to new understandings otherwise and often missed. The monthly performance and budget review is an essential meeting. It's here the learning and growing continues. Yes, the prior two sentences are repeated from earlier deliberately.

* * *

Using the budget is key.

* * *

Our budget is now elaborate in its detail. However, it began quite simply, and we have continued to expand it from there. We even add categories and items during the year as we grow and do new things. Metaphorically, it starts as a small, single-room structure and now has both curb appeal and inside upgrades galore.

Start with a basic monthly budget of only a few line items of high-level revenues and costs. Continue intensely and deliberately growing your budget and budgeting process by adding more detail as you progress with its use. Your organization needs its overall budget made up of individual budgets for each part. The parts of the organization likely need to know how their own budgets fit within the overall. Each part needs to understand and own its numbers and how its numbers impact the other parts' numbers.

Yes, goals and objectives are a part of the budgeting process. They can be for many things (leads, pipeline stages, changes in vendors, adding capacity, hiring, etc.) quite separate from, yet contributing along the way to, the organization's budget and actual results.

The words *goals* and *objectives* are often used interchangeably. For our purposes, a *goal* is usually a number or set of numbers. An *objective* is what gets accomplished when the numbers are reached. As an example, the sales goal is $100,000 for the month. The objective is to increase sales in the period. The two different words help explain different dimensions of the same event. The objective is increasing sales. The dollar amount is the goal. Increasing sales is the objective when hiring a new sales person. The new sales person could be given a monthly sales goal of $10,000.

* * *

All parts need goals and objectives.

* * *

There should be goals and objectives for every part of the organization. It's the expectations and anticipation created by goals and objectives that stimulate focus and motivate intensity. Reporting provides the results and reviewing reports drives assessments and adjustments of goals and objectives.

b. Key Performance Metrics (KPMs)

Every unit of the organization needs its own dashboard with a variety of both financial and operational measurements. Financial measurements should come from the same system as the three financial reports described at the start of the chapter. Operational measurements come from the operational activities of the organization. The term **dashboard** is used to identify a select few of the metrics that are used most often to give a quick or summarized view of the unit's performance. The dashboard should display condition and direction.

The following reports are assigned as the primary focus for leaders/managers of the functional operating parts of the organization. The principal leading and managing team may only view some of these reports on a weekly or monthly schedule, but others need to be engaged with making them happen daily and/or hour by hour. Following are the dashboard items for our organization which you can use as examples while creating yours:

Daily
- Financials
    - Cash flow
    - Cash flow projected
    - Earned revenue
    - Major variable expenses
- New subscribers
    - By entry point
    - By source
    - By theme
- Existing subscribers
    - Added users

96

- o Upgrades within suites
- o Addition of new suites
- o Onboarding pipeline
- o Training pipeline
- o Nurturing pipeline
- New Certified Coaches
  - o By entry point
  - o By source
  - o By theme
- Existing Certified Coaches
  - o Added tools
  - o Added organizations
  - o Added teams
  - o Onboarding pipeline
  - o Training pipeline
  - o Nurturing pipeline
- Website
  - o Traffic stats by page
- Alliance partners
  - o Contributions
  - o Needs

Weekly
- Cumulative reports of the dailies
- Contact center performance stats
  - o Subscribers
  - o Certified Coaches

Monthly
- Profit and loss actual versus budget
- Cash flow actual versus budget
- Balance sheet actual versus budget
- Next month projections

- Status of major Initiatives in functional areas
- Projected major Initiatives in functional areas
- Cost accounting – Knowing the margins of products and services is central to success.

The above list is not all the reports used in the organization. These are the reports used for leading and managing activities. There are many other reports providing details within functional areas and special projects. It provides a general overview of the measurements required to lead and manage our organization. These are used by the various parts of the organization.

These are also examples for you to use in establishing your lists. Each part has its own dashboard. I'll leave it up to you to determine which parts should have each of the above items on their dashboard. Each part will also have many other measurements. The ones above are just the primary ones.

The leader of each part should be able to understand and teach others about their dashboard. The requirement to teach forces individuals to learn more and understand more deeply. The ability to explain the reasons for and insights provided by each number marks the exceptional leader. Having a team equally capable of explaining the reasons and insights provided is even more important. Keeping the big picture in clear focus while giving intense attention to the details is essential to build and use your dashboard.

c. Reporting – ZL Measurements Suite

The **ZL Measurements Suite** is a set of online tools located at the website www.Zynity.com. (ZL is an abbreviation for Zynity Leadership™.) I use this suite to keep track of all the various details about the many reports created and used by all parts of the organization. Demos of this suite of tools is available at the website. The content shared in this suite of tools is for sharing the top issues required to measure and manage the activities and growth of the organization. All issues are shared in headline and story format throughout the tools.

> **As you know, website development is a constant process of updates. Rather than show you a screen shot of this tool, it's preferable for you to go to the website www.Zynity.com and see it in its current form and style.**

The primary tool in this suite is the M2G-Metrics™. This is an acronym representing the name "Measure to Grow Metrics." The report has many dimensions. In its simplest form it's an exhaustive list of all the reports grouped within categories. Examples of the categories are financial, accounting, marketing, sales, and many more.

Most of the information placed in this tool already exists in your organization. It just doesn't exist in one place in a documented form. I've asked many leaders of organizations if they have a list and description of all the reports used in their organizations and seldom do any say yes.

Getting the list and the report content in a usable and accessible form changes how we understand the reports and how we use them. It also identifies missing content, making it easier to be added into the mix. This new clarity changes individuals and the culture. Creating a philosophy about how reports are developed, used, and reviewed for accuracy and relevance adds much needed discipline.

Use of the tool is as simple as using email. We easily and quickly get others working in the tool as it's initiated. There is a bit of learning about which content to include in the tools. There's more learning about how to use the content after it's in the tools. This is all included in the process of adopting and adapting the tool into your operating infrastructure.

Following are the pieces of information gathered for each report:
- Primary elements
- Purpose
- Publishing schedule
- Publisher
- Status
- Last reviewed
- Reviewer team
- Distribution list
- Last updated

Primary elements are the points of information included in the report.
Purpose is the reason and objectives for creating the report.

Publishing schedule is the frequency of producing the report.

Publisher is the person or department responsible for creating and distributing the report.

Status notes if the report is active, in development, or dormant.

Last reviewed is the date it was last assessed and evaluated by the designated team of reviewers.

Reviewer team is the group of individuals designated to review and assess how well the report is being prepared, used, and accomplishing its purpose.

Distribution list is the names and locations of individuals sent the report on its schedule.

Last updated is the date in which changes were made to the report or any of the above items.

More pieces may be added to the above list as required by your organization.

A disciplined process of reviewing and continually refining reports in the dashboards isn't nearly as common as it should be. This added discipline in organizations transforms how each recipient of a report respects it. Knowing there is oversight, an embedded set of principles, and specific expectations for its use conveys a sense of its value. It's more than the equivalent of yesterday's sports scores. It informs one about the past with an expectation it provides information to help improve their present and future performance.

It's much more than just the numbers appearing in the reports. It's also about the way numbers are collected and presented, their purpose, and their contribution to the performance of every person who receives them.

Each number represents the results of many individuals and resources. Knowing the numbers connects individuals within and between the areas and enhances their need and ability to work together better.

Summary

Measuring the right things at the right time and sharing them properly for the purposes of guiding behavior is foundational to every organization. The more thoughtfully, deliberately, and completely this is done, the better will be individual and group performance.

The basic financial reports measure profit or margins, cash availability, and the value of the organization. There is opportunity with many organizations for the leading and managing team to use this group of reports better.

The basic operational reports are needed for each functional area to know how well they are performing and producing. Developing a process and culture of frequently reviewing and continually updating these reports leads to better results. There should be no end to the improvement of the quality and proper use of these reports. Ongoing improvement is not time-consuming once the disciplines and structure of the tools are in place.

Leading is marked by doing "right things." Managing is marked by doing "things right." Much of a leader's role is managing. Some of a manager's role is leading. Both require the proper use of measurements and the related reports.

Success is neither magical
nor mysterious.
Success is the natural consequence
of consistently applying
the basic fundamentals.

—Jim Rohn

8. Resources

Without which nothing works

Individuals, processes, and technology are the key ingredients required for the organization to breathe and grow. Dealing with each one of these ingredients properly will help even a marginal business perform well above its potential. Doing these poorly will sabotage an otherwise marvelous business. The sophistication with which an organization creates and nurtures these ingredients is more important than the quality of the business model. Even if your business model isn't all it should be, developing these key ingredients properly will result in a much-improved performance.

Adherence to the teaching in the first seven chapters of this book will provide greater results if these ingredients are solidly in place. Leaving this set of discussions until last is done to ensure it's not forgotten. It's also provided to give it distinct due attention.

a. Capital

This section is written with the assumption it's for a going concern and not a start-up. There are myriad types of monies from the three primary sources: investors, loans, and internally generated funds created from the daily operations of the business. Each source requires its own understanding and nurturing. Getting and keeping cash available for the organization is essential. Without cash the operations stop.

Chapter seven describes the reporting and monitoring needed to keep cash flowing properly in an operating organization. This is where the internally generated funds are created. How well the organization generates cash impacts significantly the organization's ability to get equity or loans as needed additional capital. This should be the first and dominant focus of the leading and managing team.

For ongoing organizations, getting and keeping cash flowing requires a team including internal individuals and accounting processes along with external individuals and processes to ensure accounting is done correctly. Principal leaders and leading and managing teams can enhance this process by understanding all dimensions of this set of the required activities. It pays to create the disciplines presented in Chapter 7 above about measurements. These disciplines and structure are foundational for all funding sources.

Getting initial, new, and additional funding is often a very difficult thing to accomplish. Each of these is a very large topic and covered separately in the eleventh book in the *A Framework for Leading*™ series, which is subtitled "Start-ups." Following is a brief overview of how the framework can help in the process of attracting investors.

All well-run organizations develop a business plan to guide what they're going to do. I recommend *Mitch's Pocket Guide to a Great Business Plan* by Mitchell Bolnick. This book builds a strong conceptual understanding needed to create a business plan. It's also very helpful as an ongoing reference resource while updating or revising a business plan on a regular basis.

The business' plan is also necessary to attract investors or get loans from a lender. This is especially necessary for those seeking funding from outside sources such as Angels or Venture Capitalists. In that plan are descriptions of the product or service, the organization, the market, and how they plan to go to market and create revenue. Following are their primary considerations.

Consideration 1: Outside funding sources first must like the idea as presented in the business plan as well as the history (accomplishments and financials) of the organization. They are very interested in yours and their estimates of the "rising tide" environment and potential of the products or services for growth or other use of the funds. There is a common sense that a rising tide will float all or most boats. This offers a better chance for creating value and/or paying off debt.

Consideration 2: The next most important thing the outside funding sources are concerned about is the qualifications and experience of the leading and managing team. They rely on their history and credentials to give them confidence they can make their plan happen.

* * *

New information to help get funding

* * *

New Consideration 3: Completing the template in this book and having a documented framework adds another dimension to build confidence with funding sources. The entrepreneurial team should come with their leading and managing document explaining how they are going to lead and manage the business daily, weekly, and monthly. This is a concept becoming even more popular as more organizations adopt this methodology and the online tools. In addition to past successes bolstering credentials, the funding sources will be eager to see there is definition and clarity for the leading and managing tasks and opportunities ahead.

b. Individuals

Attracting, selecting, engaging, encouraging, inspiring, mentoring, and developing individuals marks the exceptional organizations. All the above steps are of equal importance.

Quality documented Human Resource policies and procedures are best developed with the aid of an outside professional individual or firm that is doing this for many others in your state as well as for you. Get it started and underway as soon as possible.

Working with each person to define and document what is expected of them is just a start. Continuing to monitor and adjust this document is necessary for it to stay fresh. It's about more than the rules. It's about devoting time to individuals. A set of shared or opposing attitudes will spill over into how you and they treat one another and your customers as well. Individuals work better when they know what is expected of them with measurements in place to confirm and affirm their results.

* * *

Each individual is valuable.

* * *

Everyone should have an individual development plan containing a statement of who they are becoming and how they plan to get there. This is just as important for those planning to evolve themselves out of your organization as those who are planning to stay.

Everyone should also have an individual profile document describing who they are and how they got there. This should include their accomplishments, experiences, assessments, key milestones, and a statement of how they perceive themselves.

Both the development plan and the profile may have some items to be kept personal and private. There should also be significant parts of the profile and the plan developed to be shared with selected others. These selected others should be chosen carefully.

Individuals are the most important ingredient/asset in the organization. Deliberately and overtly treating them properly proves their worth in your organization and in the world. Compensation plans are critical and should reflect leadership's respect and concern for each individual.

* * *

The title *individual* is important.

* * *

I use the term *individual* deliberately rather than people. Words make a difference. They reflect our view or perception. They also reflect our thoughts, attitudes, and motives that show up in our behavior.

I refer to those who contribute to our organization as talented individuals or TIs for short. I respect each one as the talented individual they are. The label TI reflects the full set of positive thoughts, attitudes, and motives I feel toward them. The label keeps this foremost in my mind. Some are external to the organization as independent agents. Some are internal as official employees with all the rights, responsibilities, and privileges afforded that relationship.

In its worst connotation, the label "people" conveys a sense (thoughts, attitudes, and motives) of an indistinguishable gray mass or herd. In its worst connotation, the label "employee" conveys both a sense of ownership by one party and paid servitude by the other party.

I avoid use of the words *employee*, *associate*, and *people* as much as possible. I hear them often in conversations where one is referring to them when in conversation with a third party not attached to the organization. I suggest you adopt the label TI and stop using the other labels completely. It'll help you reinforce your best thoughts, attitudes, and motives about all the talented individuals you get to collaborate with daily.

When TIs work together of their own individual passionate will to fulfill their role, they produce contributions they each deem important. It begins with how we all perceive and respect one another.

- Each TI comes to our organization with high expectations for themselves and the organization.
- Each TI is different.
- Each TI has many talents.
- Each TI must be able to provide their own ignition (self-starting) and self-discipline.
- Each TI comes equipped to learn, bear down, and contribute to winning as a team.

TIs are motivated mostly by how their contributions add value to others. Encouraging this attitude increases the strength of the organization's culture. Helping them measure this increases the impact of acknowledging their contributions. It's worth the effort even if the measurements aren't perfect.

* * *

Professional engagement standards

* * *

Establishing and adhering to a set of **professional engagement standards** enhances individual and organizational worth and performance. Many of these items are included in and woven within the cultures of organizations. Following are a few ideas to help you create your own so you can bring them with you in all the places you go:

- Have respect for others always.
- Treat others just as or more important than you.
- Others' well-being is a priority.
- Be a great learner.
- Strive to be a great teacher.
- Give benefit of the doubt in all circumstances.
- Always offer to help when you can.
- Be sensitive and thoughtful.
- Keep the big picture in focus always.

TIs are multidimensional. Each one has depth and breadth of talent, personality, and character. It's good to invest time exploring and understanding the many dimensions of each one. Organizations should engage the use of professionals to do a variety of individual assessments and teach everyone about the process and value of each assessment.

The Zynity online tools have a place to post the results for each person so they can be readily available to others. This helps everyone use the results of the assessments to know one another better and consider each individual's many dimensions.

All the above is helped significantly by having a focus on creating and living within a clear and defined culture. Building the culture is a key priority. Each organization has its value system and sense of priorities.

Document, assess, and measure these to grow richness and depth in your culture with positive impact for everyone.

c. Processes

Respecting this as its own identifiable category as a resource is essential. It deserves its own living identity. Documenting, assessing, and refining processes is not an optional discipline. Processes reflect the need to perform some tasks in a repeatable manner. The growing use of process disciplines highlight its role in improving the delivery of all types of services to customers and clients.

A substantial contributor for improving operations is the use of Six Sigma. It is a highly regarded discipline with training and certifications for individuals. It's available throughout the world. It began at Motorola in 1986 and has flourished from those roots. A search of the term Six Sigma will reveal its growing pervasive role and contributions.

Six Sigma began as a structured discipline to reduce errors in processes of manufacturing. It has come to be recognized as a dominant encourager and discipline for the use of documented processes. It establishes structure for creating processes correctly. The result is significantly improved operations throughout organizations. It's okay to obsess a bit about having, adhering to, and measuring the outcomes from processes. Get on board with this fast moving and value-laden train.

Documented processes are essential.

Growth of **business process management (BPM)** and **business process outsourcing (BPO)** professional organizations is another testimony to the importance of processes in the operations of well-run organizations. These terms are frequently used interchangeably. It's all about using specific disciplines with business processes to accomplish delivery of a specific capability such as contact centers, segments of supply chains for manufacturers, and third-party billing services.

It is clear the reliance upon and sophistication of developing processes is increasing. This helps everyone think in more disciplined ways to express operational activities in clear and well-defined steps with measurements. The use of documented processes doesn't restrict or dampen creativity. Their use increases creativity and makes innovation easier. It's very encouraging to see the growing body of knowledge and applied techniques improving their development and use.

Don't launch or operate your organization without heavy use of process development. Leaders and managers should be very familiar with its value. Bring certified Six Sigma individuals onto your staff, get some of your staff Six Sigma certified, or hire outsourced Six Sigma professionals to lead and do this for you.

d. Technology

Technology platforms, packages, and programs of all types and uses are being adopted everywhere. Even for small and midsize organizations there are packages available for use of computers and smart phones for every part and function of the organization. They range from accounting to customer relationship to project management and to all parts for collaboration and disciplined sharing of information.

No organization should operate without this readily available technology. There should be (or at least a specific plan for) a package with operating instructions for every part of the organization. (Refer back to the **operational organization chart** in Chapter 4 to see again how we use them at Zynity.)

There is no end in sight to the increasing availability of technology to support every activity throughout the organization. This changes everything. Individuals adapt, opportunities open, and customers engage with your organization's technology more easily on a daily growing basis.

An appropriate business rule is to adopt technology and change to new evolutions of technology as quickly as possible. This requires plans and the adjustment of these plans on a frequent basis. A competitor coming at you leveraging the latest technology is a real threat. Get there ahead of them.

e. Outside professionals

The use of outside professionals in supportive roles on an as-needed basis is growing. This was common in the past for such specialized services as legal and marketing. The list has been expanded to include:

- Leadership coaches
- Management coaches
- Boards
- Complete human resources departments
- Finance and accounting
- Processes
- Design and engineering
- Information technology
- Distribution
- And many more …

Some industries have very specialized individuals not included in the above categories. In all cases, be open to receive and act upon input. One of the best ways to demonstrate how smart you are, is being very coachable. This fits very well with a willingness to work harder than most.

Outsourcing is growing. Manufacturing organizations, for example, outsource as many of the pieces of their products as possible. This allows them to engage specialists who have their own leadership and operations capabilities and core competencies. This allows organizations to get better at providing specifications and assessing the quality of results. It encourages them to focus on their own core competencies.

Summary

Being deliberately focused and disciplined with the use of resources establishes a solid and consistent foundation upon which all parts of the organization can grow. This consistency makes it easier for the parts to work together better. Individuals are important.

Processes and technology expand and extend the capacities of the organization and its individuals. Yes, everything should be updated as a matter of course, but having these capabilities prominently in place makes everything easier.

It's a lost opportunity when organizations don't invest deliberate attention to define and clarify their principles, policies, strategies, and activities within these resources. Doing this very well adds to the flexibility and capacity for organizations to grow at accelerated rates. This gives access to additional resources with short notice. It allows bringing on new individuals and getting them up to speed more quickly. It enhances the ability to get and keep everyone engaged with their specific responsibilities along with a big-picture perspective. This adds importance to the grand purpose for which the organization exists. It helps everyone celebrate and share in what the organization is accomplishing.

*I've never really tried to copy anyone;
I like to have my own style.*

—Liam Aiken

Do It Your Way

Everyone has a personal way and style to lead and manage their organization. Getting others to engage with you and stay on the same page isn't easy. Expressing your way in a clear and simple document is necessary for others to buy into it, fully contribute within it, and help you continue refining it.

Why? Once others can buy into and contribute to your way of leading and managing, they'll align with the shared purpose and priorities and work together better. Overall performance will improve greatly. So, do it your way, but make a deliberate effort to fully engage your team. Begin with the outline provided in this book and you will describe "Your Way."

In this process, you'll get to know yourself more clearly and deeply. This deeper understanding and the process will motivate and guide you to express yourself more clearly and accurately. This will be received by others as a positive statement of your integrity and build respect for your transparency.

* * *

Define – Document – Clarify – Refine™

* * *

This book presumes you don't have a fully defined and documented outline describing how you lead and manage your organization. It's intended to help you remedy this omission to improve the way you do things.

Everyone on a leading and managing team needs to actively engage with defining, documenting, clarify, and continually refining how they lead and manage. This builds clarity, discipline, and accelerated performance for you and those with whom you work.

* * *

Creating is easier with a model or template.

* * *

Creating almost anything is easier if there is a template or model to follow. It's also easier to edit and adjust an existing document than having to start with a blank page and create from there. This book presents a template for you to use as an outline and model for defining and expressing your framework. It evolves one step at a time on your own schedule.

The steps become a way to reveal and exhibit your personal leadership approach and style. The objective is to have the steps result in a document in which you describe your leading and managing framework.

The word **framework** is used here as the essential overarching **structure** to describe and support your way of leading and managing, providing boundaries, definitions, and clarity. This is needed to establish discipline, consistency, and harmony. The words **framework** and **structure** are sometimes used interchangeably throughout the book.

The framework establishes the boundaries and guidelines for shaping the dimensions of leading and managing activities in an organization. Each organization has its own boundaries and guidelines, and it's essential to document and adhere to them in a disciplined manner.

Once the basics of your framework are documented, it's easy to continue adding, editing, and improving it. Engage your team in this process from the beginning. It takes a village. Morale will be lifted significantly. Leading and managing is a team sport. Life and work gets easier and more productive for everyone just knowing the framework's underway and evolving. Everyone learns together.

This is good for organizations in various stages. It helps start-ups plan and prepare how they'll operate the business from its beginning. It's also good for existing organizations eager to accelerate growth. They will conduct their daily activities with excellence while building habits and clear definitions for the future.

Use the samples and examples provided in the outline of this book to stimulate your own development. Start by adding a single sentence of your content in each topic of the outline. The document grows on its own from there and the magic begins to appear.

Edit and add to the outline to suit your organization and style. The right answers and correct content are what you determine them to be. You will continue editing it forever (life evolves) so don't get too hung up on a single item. Just write it. Everything can always be improved later.

*A company could put a top
person at every position
and be swallowed by a competitor
with people only half as good,
but who are working together.*

—W. Edwards Deming

You Know It's Working When...

You will know all of this is working when every member of the leading and managing team (and the talented supervisory individuals – your next leaders and mangers) are asking these questions of themselves and others throughout each day:

(1) Am I/are we working and spending our time on the right things? (leading)

(2) Am I/are we doing things right in the best possible way? (managing)

(3) Is what I'm doing working well with what all the others are doing? (leverage)

This level of awareness, introspection, and perspective transforms organizations. Your role is to nurture this in your environment, so everyone has a vibrant and rewarding life making contributions in the organization you all love.

*The most rewarding things
you do in life are
often the ones that look like
they cannot be done.*

—Arnold Palmer

Apply What You Document

A Model

Many of us easily relate to sports and enjoy the thrills of participating and spectating. We hear often about the systems of very successful coaches. A great system is necessary for one to be a successful coach at any level. A defined system makes it easier for all the participants to understand their roles, so they can all work together better.

We want to help leading and managing systems become as common in small, midsize, and parts of larger organizations as they are with sports teams. This book, related methodology, and online tools are designed specifically to make it easy for leaders and managers to develop and execute with their own framework. The objective is to increase organizational effectiveness.

The Outline of Your Document

The eight segments of the outline are as follows:

(1) Philosophy
(2) What we do
(3) Our organization
(4) The markets we serve
(5) New ways, new things
(6) Everyone customer focused at all times
(7) Eyes on the numbers in all parts
(8) Resources

Individuals and organizations who follow the outline to create their own document and implement it in their organization can make the following statements with confidence:

(1) I'm clear and able to express how I lead and manage and why I do it.

(2) Why we do what we do matters to us and all the stakeholders we serve. We make a difference to all those in the world we touch.

(3) Our organization is structured to produce optimally and use our resources effectively.

(4) The individuals we serve have specific needs. Our contributions help them do what they do better.

(5) We continually improve what we do and how we do it. Innovation stimulates us. We make new things happen rather than just talking about them.

(6) We've specifically designed how our organization works around how we attract, engage, and serve our customers and clients.

(7) We measure and review everything we do to lead, manage, and operate our organization.

(8) We use all our resources effectively. We engage outside professionals to help us and teach us in various parts of our organization.

The above is accomplished while doing your regular daily activities within your organization with your team members. It quickly becomes fun and engages everyone with notable improvements to celebrate. Doing your regular work in slightly new ways gets easy to do very quickly. New things are added as needed over time.

Doing this with your real-life teammates, using your organization's real information, makes it practical and more effective. No need to go offsite to a weeklong session while hoping to remember what you're taught so you can bring it back and teach others. At best, this is a shotgun approach to improving the organization's leading and managing capabilities.

* * *

The outline frames the document.

* * *

Developing your fully written outline should be spread out over a few months. It takes a while, which makes it less intrusive. It's a bit of work, but worth it. No one becomes a United States Navy SEAL watching videos and reading the manual. There is no magic pill or single idea that will transform how your organization functions. It takes doing right things in the right way. Completing this outline and applying the related methodology and online tools will transform your organization's environment and how it functions.

There are eight separate chapters in this book presenting samples of the basic information for each of these eight segments. The segments are presented in their most basic form with actual samples of content used in a live organization. The content in these chapters are examples only, but they represent the types of content you need to establish and use in your organization.

If there's interest in expanding your understanding of this model, there's a series of related books, *A Framework for Leading*™, which teaches more about the methodology. Our *Zynity Leadership™* (ZL) online tools are available at www.zynity.com and are specifically designed to help you apply this methodology. The methodology and the online tools used together help you construct your own framework using the content and activities of your organization.

Online training to become certified in using the methodology is available at the Framework for Leading Institute (www.F4LI.com). The courses are designed for students to progress at their own pace. When all members of a leading and managing team are certified, their ability to work together is enhanced significantly. It's the same advantage experienced when software developers work together on a project using the same platform and tools.

Some of what is presented here exists in many larger organizations. It's often referred to as their "operating infrastructure." Many small and midsize organizations don't have the needed infrastructure in place. The methodology in this book is designed to help build and extend the needed infrastructure.

We get you started with a framework within which a solid and scalable infrastructure can be established. Infrastructure allows operating more effectively and growing more easily. Without structure, definition, and clarity everything requiring change is more difficult. Ongoing change is essential for growth.

As you read a printed or digital version of the book, add your underlines, comments, and questions in the book as they occur. This is a resource for you to use as a template for creating your own infrastructure. It's all about how this is valuable to you, your organization, and the individuals who contribute to it.

Following the template and teaching in this book and its related materials will help leading and managing teams develop and continue refining their how-they'll-make-it-happen documented plan. Having a great product or service is important. Demonstrating operating excellence makes the ultimate difference.

* * *

The document leads to operating excellence.

* * *

An exciting example of demonstrating operating excellence is what Steve Kerr did in his interview with the Golden State Warriors leadership when he applied to be their head coach. He had no experience as a head coach. He had a very successful career in the NBA as a player. He did bring a large, well-thought-out and documented plan to show how he was going to *make it happen*. And, he did. They won the Championship in his first year as their head coach. In the second year they won more games (73–9) in a single season than any team in the history of the NBA.

The Warriors were in the playoffs again in 2016. It was only Coach Kerr's second year. They lost in the last minutes of the seventh game by only four points. Yes, the team is still playing at an extremely high level. Everyone credits everyone else for the success to be inclusive as they should. Kerr's how-we-will-do-it defined plan certainly helped everyone be better. It has now helped other teams also be better. It raised the bar and introduced new knowledge. Teams need the harmony created by a written leadership plan. Definition creates clarity and reduces chaos and distractions. It makes harmony possible with every individual engaged with one another and the organization.

Coach Kerr will continue refining his system. He'll add new players and new ideas. He will likely never again create from scratch the full go-make-it-happen documented plan. He'll just keep adding, editing, and refining the one he began with. It would be fun to see how much of the original plan remains by the end of his tenth season. You get the points; document, experience, learn, refine, and continue repeating.

Coach Kerr never needs to start over writing his plan. But he has a framework and document to continue refining. He, no doubt, makes changes every week. Remember, the external (competition) and internal (team members) pieces keep changing and adapting to your changes.

We want this for you. Build your own written leading and managing plan. Keep refining it.

The will to win,
the desire to succeed,
the urge to reach your full potential?
These are the keys that will unlock
the door to personal excellence.

—Eddie Robinson

Grow and Develop

Growing an organization isn't easy. Developing as a leader and manager isn't a cakewalk either. This book is an invitation to adopt a methodology, along with its online tools, to make the growing and developing easier.

The broad definition of the following two words with very different meanings is done early so we can begin with a clear and shared understanding:

> LEADING: Future and right things.

> MANAGING: Present and things right.

One can readily get that I have added the words future and present to Peter Drucker's famous quotes about management and leadership. The use of *things* carries with it the broadest inclusion of all activities associated with either very distinct verb. As we continue you will grasp fully why I've added the time dimension to these words.

Leaders must be contemplating the future to establish right things. Managers must be focused on the present to ensure things are done right. Leaders and managers in most organizations do both all the time and switch between them without taking the time to consciously detect or reflect on which one they're doing. It's okay. However, there must be intentional times set aside to do them consciously as well.

There are countless quotes and books on leadership and just as many or more about management. Using a simple definition for both words allows us to communicate more effectively than if we attempted to account for all nuances. We use *leading* and *managing* and their variances often. Please use the above definitions as broadly as intended in all cases whether in verb or noun form.

It is popular and proper to expect leadership to guide their organizations to
    (1) work on the right things
    (2) nurture a supportive culture in which all individuals can flourish.
    (3) ensure effective and efficient use of all available resources.
Leadership must have its own defined, coordinated, and adaptable structure within which it accomplishes all three to create optimal results.

This book introduces the *need for* and *how to* establish more structure in leading and managing small and midsize organizations. It presents a simple, easy, and effective way to develop and operate with more structure. Adaptable structure makes life easier and more productive for everyone. It also stimulates a focus on preventive rather than remedial attention to problems.

This book invites you to an adventure. It guides you in a process to create clarity about how you lead and manage your organization or your part of the organization. While your clarity is being created, it helps you establish your own adaptable structure. It also engages you with others on your team, so they are doing it with you. Leading and managing is a team activity. It's about individuals coming together to accomplish a greater good for all those they serve.

Leadership is quite often associated with personality and presence. We're suggesting adding a well-formed structure for leading and managing will enhance results significantly.

Why you should do this?

- Create more successes
- Communicate more effectively
- Reduce stress
- Extend capacities
- Expand capabilities
- Increase margins
- Have more fun

Leading and managing isn't easy.

Building a successful and high-performing organization is rare. Yet there are many who work very hard to do it. The processes in this adventure add structure and define ways to engage with others. Completing this adventure increases significantly the likelihood of building your organization to be all you've expected and need it to be. Building requires an obvious solid foundation and a prominent framework. Without both, it is impossible to get the other necessary parts to fit and work together efficiently and effectively for any length of time.

To keep this personal and practical, I share, in the following parts of the book, my actual information. This book expresses and documents how I lead and manage my company, Zynity, LLC. It's designed to serve as a working and living example for you to use as a guide to create your own foundation and framework. It must be customized by you to suit your style and your organization. I make changes to this often.

The adventure will continue. Each member of the leading and managing team is guided to begin documenting and structuring how they lead and manage their primary area and connect with each other. Once the documenting and structuring have started, the refining will continue and include ongoing input from others.

Addressing the opportunities

The opportunities/problem(s) addressed in this book are an extensive list of issues aggravated by the lack of structure in leading and managing. The amounts and diversity of dysfunction caused by the absence of structure are well known by those working in organizations. Just ask around, write down your own observations, and you will create your own local list. This is not the place to itemize the list. This is the place to address and begin implementing a solution.

Experience and knowledge

Experience is the best teacher. Knowledge is power. These two statements are acknowledged as truths by almost everyone. I agree to some extent. However, when we say them, we must also include the qualifiers, even if unspoken, that these truths are very dependent on the individual. If we don't actively and deliberately learn from the experiences we have, then we may not learn all we should. If we don't use and apply the knowledge we accumulate correctly and fully, the impact of its power is diminished. So, maybe we should alter what we say with "experience can be the best teacher" and "knowledge provides the potential for great power." This book and its related materials and activities are designed to help us intentionally *learn* from our experiences and *apply* what we know, so they may have their maximum impact.

Let the fun begin.

It is exciting. Let's get underway helping your organization provide a more rewarding and vibrant work environment for everyone. More structure in leading and managing brings increased productivity with less stress.

This book also introduces a series of books, *A Framework for Leading*™, in which is presented a way to improve leading and managing in organizations of all types. It includes online training to help use the framework's methodology and the related *Zynity Leadership*™ (ZL) online tools. It begins with establishing structure and processes for communicating at the top level. The disciplines created extend to all levels. A related network of *Certified Coaches* makes implementing this easier.

The result: **individuals working together in harmony!**

A mindset that understands order, is a mindset that can understand leadership.

—Wayne Chirisa

Leadership Styles

Your mix of styles matters.

Your style matters. I have observed, while working with many companies, the most frequent styles of leading and managing can be characterized as follows: (1) The Machete™, (2) The Spinning Plates™, and (3) The Toy Box™. These three behavior styles exist in varying percentages in all individuals in leading and managing roles.

The Machete™ is characterized by the movie images of an explorer lost in a jungle or tangle of issues and attempting to whack their way through them with a large thick and curved sword. This style appears most frequently on Monday mornings. The Spinning Plates™ is characterized by the movie images of a very busy and intense person running from one spinning plate on a pole to another as the spinning is waning and they rush to keep it spinning. The Toy Box™ is characterized by the movie images of a very eager person arriving in a room full of toys and deciding to play with the toy they are most attracted to at that moment. It's also known in some circles as the avoidance phenomenon. These styles will always exist in varying emphases with growing organizations. They are all needed in right proportions.

One thing common in all three styles presented above is the drug of choice in their organizations, which is known as "busyness." There is a sense of being busy without considering if the busy is with the right things. Addiction to the drug is begun with the assumption: if we get real busy, and stay real busy, we'll get a lot done, and good things will happen. Busyness can be a virtue and it can also be a problem. Busyness with wrong things isn't a virtue. It's important to get *focused* on right things before you get busy. This is an essential requirement for leading, managing, evolving, and growing organizations.

This book and its related materials are designed to help you put in place the much needed fourth style of leading and managing: (4) The Airline Pilot™. This style is noted for its order, calmness, deliberateness, and checklists. While pilots are on their way to the airport, specific preparations are underway by prepared and organized teams. Once at the airport, the briefing times cover all the big issues: time, destination, resources, and participants. Settling into the cockpit requires viewing another set of gauges and checklists. This settled style brings comfort and focus to the crew.

The Airline Pilot™ style needs to be added and nurtured in your organization if you expect to do the right things, in the right way, in the right sequence. The percentage of this style must increase as the organization gets larger. This will be explained further in the next chapter.

The information and exercises in this book are specifically designed to help you get more prepared and focused. It assumes you will have to stay busy, but with the right things, in the right amount, and in the right sequence. You will exhibit all four styles in the right proportions and right times for your organization.

*Growth is never by mere chance;
it is the result of forces
working together.*

—James Cash Penney

Growth Stages

The evolving focus of leading and managing

Growing an organization isn't easy. Each stage of growth requires a different focus and set of leading and managing skills. Awareness and clarity about the focus and skills needed is essential to being successful in each stage and evolving to the next stage. This book will help.

Knowing which stage you are in and the steps needed to get to the next place is not always so clear. There are so many details and moving parts it often seems confusing. It's essential to establish clarity as you grow. Clarity allows intentionality in developing focus and discipline.

Some say only the brave and the foolish take on the task of building and growing an organization. Others say it's the only way to live a life. In both assumptions the roles and complexities of leading and managing are the dominant focus causing aversion and excitement. A prime objective in this book is to make leading and managing more exciting and less formidable.

The chart on the next page is used to explain, in simple terms, the three most common stages in the life of an organization. It also includes an explanation of the focus needed for leading and managing an organization in each stage and the changes required to grow to the next stage. There are many other such charts pertaining to organizational growth with much more detail. Keeping it simple here is deliberate. Yet it still takes a bit to explain.

Leading and Managing Focus at each Stage

	Operations	Organization	Enterprise
# of Leaders:	1 – 2	3 – 4	5 +
Behavior:	Supervisor	Manager	Leader
Time Focus:	Day-Week	Week-Month	Quarter-Year
	Tasks	Individuals	Managing Team
	Tactics	Processes	Strategies
	Product	Technology	Customers
	Activities	Functions	Measurements

A Framework for Leading™

Let's turn our attention to understanding the stage of development of your organization. Please look at the chart above and assess which stage you're in. Clarifying which stage you are in will help you assess the correctness of how you're doing and what you're doing. You may need a bit more of the information contained in this chapter to finalize your thoughts on which stage you're in. Some may be in a bit of more than one which is expected. Understanding these three main stages will also help you identify what you need to do to get to the next stage.

It is important to agree, at the outset, it's not required for all organizations to go to the next stage. There are millions of **Operations** stage businesses making great contributions to their communities, employees, and owners. Some products and services are best provided in Operations stage organizations.

It is also important to recognize that as an organization evolves to the next stage, the characteristics and behaviors of the prior stage are also needed. The requirement of getting to the next stage is the adopting of new capabilities that help you do the prior stage activities even more effectively. For example, being even more customer focused in the **Enterprise** stage forces the increased attention on activities required for the products/services in the primary stage. The needs and contributions of the **Organization** stage are even more important as the organization evolves to a next stage.

The content of this book is designed to help organizations in each stage do what they do better and with more enjoyment and successes. It also addresses the needs of others who want to grow their businesses, but don't have a model and/or template for putting in place the necessary ingredients required at the next stages of growth.

Each stage requires an expanded (broader and deeper) view of how to get things done in an organization. While in a stage, it's okay to stay focused with its requirements. It's also appropriate to begin putting in place the basics of the requirements and elements needed to get to the next stage.

* * *

Operations Stage

* * *

The Operations stage requires that the leader behave in a manner much like a supervisor level in a larger organization. They are often very involved with basic activities along with the other doers.

The time focus is *what we're doing at the moment,* so we can complete the day's scheduled work. Learning time is short. Mistakes can be fixed quickly. The excitement created with seeing things get done happens often and feeds a need for a sense of accomplishment.

Attention to tasks and the tactics to get things completed is necessary. The main event is seeing the product or service delivered to the end user. Almost everyone participates in all the activities required to build and sell the products/services. Hands on. It's about details and guidelines.

* * *

Organization Stage

* * *

The Organization stage requires that the leader behave in a manner much like a manager level in a larger organization. There are also occasions when it's necessary for the leader to behave as a supervisor as well. It's primarily a focus on supervisors' activities with the doers. The infrastructure required is to formalize the operations of the organization.

The time focus is *what we need to get ready for this week and the weeks ahead.* In the past if we ran out of supplies, or had someone sick and not show up, we missed a delivery. Now we're a step or two ahead with calendar alerts and ordering processes for supplies to get prepared for what's needed for the next weeks.

Leading and managing attention is on supervisors directing individuals doing the tasks and the processes they use to do their work. Technology is a subject to consider in all the things being done. Individuals work in groups responsible for building the product or selling the product. Very few participate in both even though they collaborate. It makes it easier to manage doing each activity right. Separation of work allows for efficiencies and departments are needed. Hands off. It's about guidelines and concepts.

* * *

Enterprise Stage

* * *

The Enterprise stage requires that the leader behave in a manner much like a C-level individual in a larger organization. It's now a focus on developing leaders and managers to guide and build. The infrastructure required is to formalize the leading and managing of the organization.

There are many occasions when it's still necessary for the leader to behave as a supervisor and as a manager. However, the amount of time spent engaging in the different behaviors is what changes. Please refer to the "Leadership Styles" chapter for additional input on this.

The time focus is *what we need to accomplish this month and the months ahead*. We have a set of leaders and managers in the departments and they're scheduled to complete a defined set of deliverables.

Attention is placed on managing and developing the leading and managing team. It's a continuous cycle of assessing if individuals are doing right things and are doing them in the right way. *What* is being done is as important as *how* it's being done.

As much as we love our products or services for what they are (our creations), we now need to become even more concerned about how our customers feel about their experience with them. We give as much attention to all we're doing as we do to what our competitors are doing

146

to pull our customers into their world. We consider how the changes in the world impact the importance and place of our products or services.

We also may be separated from the daily activities, but we design measurements and reports that keep us, and other leader/managers connected with all we're doing throughout the organization. It's remote influence. It's about concepts and principles.

* * *

The Dynamics

* * *

It is important to recognize the dynamics that occur between and within each of the stages. What is done in each stage should improve as the capabilities of the next stage are added to your organization. The following diagram presents a more complete picture of the dynamics. Growing an organization without adding the next stage of required capabilities can prove to be very limiting or disastrous. These new capabilities are the foundation for scalability of leading and managing. This is essential for sustainable growth and evolving a maturing organization.

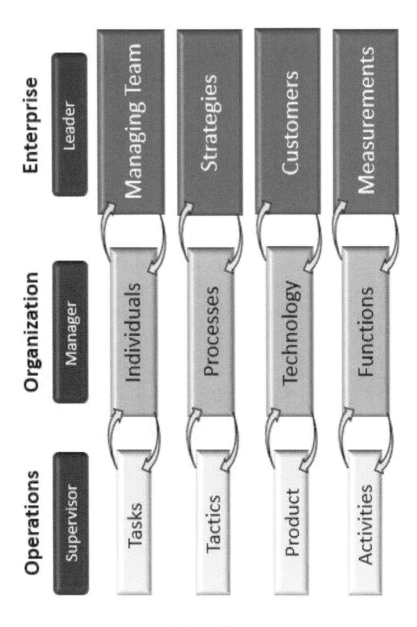

Design by Keith Burns

148

* * *

Leading and Managing Style

* * *

As you finish this chapter, I hope you will also refresh your thinking about and review the three most common styles (The Machete™, The Spinning Plates™, and The Toy Box™) and the urge to get busy and stay busy. This is the biggest barrier to progressing to the next levels. Evolving to the next stages requires more use of The Airline Pilot™ style. It's popular to continue doing more work and expecting more work. It's difficult to deliberately set aside time to think about and plan for the next things or doing things more efficiently.

You will discover it's much easier to plan for next things with structure, a methodology, and online tools to guide you in the required new thinking and processes. This is how you will start and increase using The Airline Pilot™ style in your growing organization. I've resisted providing a chart of the percentages of each style required with each stage. I hope you will build your own chart and challenge yourself along the way.

A gnarled web of barriers evolves from the nourishment received by getting very good with the requirements and styles of the first two stages. It's difficult to give up the immediate rewards received while doing them. Many leaders prefer to avoid the much more difficult process of becoming a C-level leader (The Airline Pilot™). They think it won't be fun, and their decision may be right for them. We hope this book and its related information will encourage many to take their next big steps even though it's a bit intimidating.

Summary

The stages of growing an organization along with yourself and others may seem difficult. It is not impossible. And, for some, far easier than you imagine.

It is exciting to observe that many are eager to overcome the real and perceived barriers. A more defined and structured process than "I'll figure it out as I go" is needed. The methodology and online tools incorporated in the "How You Lead and Manage" option makes it easier, more effective, and results in a greater extension of everyone's abilities, capacities, and capabilities.

Leadership is a way of thinking,
a way of acting and,
most importantly,
a way of communicating.

—Simon Sinek

The Online Tools

Having more information about the use of online tools will be very helpful to you. For the leading and managing team to be connected and aligned it's possible to adapt a variety of collaboration tools available today. They will get you some of the way to where you need to be. Their major shortcoming is they aren't designed to integrate well with the other three parts of the framework (strategies, customers, and measurements). The need is more than just collaborating about things as they are.

I'm stressing the use of online tools for a few reasons. The need for them is best illustrated by comparing Zynity's tools with other online tools. To keep it simple, I'll explain Zynity's online tools for the leading and managing team in comparison to online tools used for sales and customer relationship management (CRM).

In your organization, is the marketing and sales team more important than the leading and managing team? Of course, the answer is they are both very important. Both are vitally essential to the organization.

Consider the following:
Almost all organizations use a specifically designed online, browser-based connected set of sales and CRM tools to help all departments know more about prospects and customers. Not many years ago this was all done on paper. Now all this information is digital and virtual. Once information is in a digital state it can be used more effectively. The following are a few advantages of having the information digitally:

- Better content collection
- Improved use of content
- Increased performance and satisfaction
- Deeper awareness and analysis
- Anticipating trends
- Increased revenue
- Stronger customer relationships
- Cross-department collaboration (sales, accounting, service, operations)

Think about this:

Very few organizations use a specifically designed set of online tools to help designated parties know more about the leading and managing activities in the organization. The usual methods for collecting and sharing leading and managing information are in meetings, lists, documents, conversations, emails, or it's not shared at all. Too many ideas and relevant knowledge just stay in heads and hearts for various reasons. Some of the reasons are: it takes time to clarify thinking, there's no required place to share it, it's not the right moment to share, uncertainty of its value, and many other reasons great ideas wander and get shelved in heads and hearts.

Having a browser-based connected set of leading and managing tools helps organize and present the correct information:

- Thinking – ideas and opportunities
- Focus – where my head is now
- Issues and concerns – threats and weaknesses
- Deliverables – tangible items to produce
- Activities – events requiring my time

- Initiatives – items needed to move us forward
- Customer view – their experience with us
- Measurements – accurate and effective

The above items of information exist in most organizations, but they aren't connected in a cohesive overarching framework with a coordinated purpose, discipline, and focus. They are scattered around the organization in space and time. The Zynity online, browser-based connected set of leading and managing tools brings all that content together in a cohesive structure. Just like the improvement we experience with online sales automation, the leading and managing improvements will be seen with:

- Better content collection
- Improved visibility through centralizing content
- Increase performance and satisfaction
- Accelerated leveraging of all resources
- Revenue growth
- Tracking and anticipating trends
- Individual talent growth
- Coordinate multiple touch points (all functions)

Now the leading and managing team can have the same advantages of automation experienced by sales and customer support teams. This is a key ingredient in making the leading and managing dimension of an organization more scalable, just as automation makes the sales and customer service more scalable.

Noticeable changes in the team are:

- Intentional regular sharing
- More comprehensive perspective
- Speaking in C-level style
- More effective communicating
- Consideration of others' thinking and input
- Broader and deeper awareness
- Easier to anticipate changes and trends
- Less stress and more harmony

The above items contribute to a more open and engaged community of talented individuals. They extend their common language, learn from one another, get to key points easier, and contribute to the organization's success with less turmoil while sharing right things in the right way.

Big-picture perspective:

Often, I hear leaders say, "I wish my team could see it as I see it." They are usually talking about the desire for others to have a bigger-picture view of an opportunity or event rather than just seeing it from how it impacts their local area of responsibility. With the online tools it's easier to help others learn to ask:

- What are all the parts?
- How do they fit together?
- How can they better integrate?
- What adjustments are needed?
- Which parts need attention now?
- How do adjustments affect other parts?
- Are goals creating tension between parts?
- Where will resources have the most impact?

Learning to ask and answer these types of questions help everyone put opportunities and incidents in a big-picture perspective. Issues get addressed more quickly and effectively with less turmoil and greater successes. This is essential for organizations to function at a high-performance level and progress in growing to the next stages.

Art and science have their meeting point in method.

—Edward G. Bulwer-Lytton

The Methodology

The *Framework for Leading*™ methodology is a central component in this book, the related series of books, and the solution. It introduces the need for building a leading and managing structure on a proper understanding of and implementing the four big parts of an organization. The four big parts of the framework are:

(1) Strategies
(2) Customers
(3) Managing team
(4) Measurements

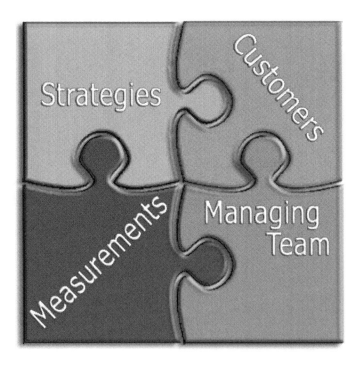

How well these four big parts are implemented in an organization determines its success. These four comprise the heart of leading and managing. Each part is essential and intertwined with the others. If you do all four of these things very well, this will establish doing many other things exceptionally well. If you do one of these big parts poorly, it creates problems for many other parts. The ripple effect is obvious here.

Great accomplishments begin with a purpose. Specific focus on goals create a journey. Seeking understanding gives clarity. Structure and planning helps utilize resources more effectively and efficiently.

Leading and managing an organization to accomplish great things isn't easy. There are many surprising twists and turns. There always seems to be a shortage of resources.

Highly effective leaders and managers can answer this basic question: *How do you lead and manage your organization?* The answer should have one-minute, five-minute, ten-minute, thirty-minute, and one-hour versions as well as a working document.

The history of this book begins with a journey to answer the above mentioned basic question. Surprisingly very few leaders and managers can answer this question clearly and simply. It's important for individuals leading and managing all areas of an organization to be able to answer how they lead and manage their part of the organization.

I use the terms *leaders* and *managers* and *leading* and *managing* together often. I do this as leaders must manage and managers must lead. They are different things and must be distinguished. However, in daily activities these must be done almost simultaneously. The accomplished practitioner doesn't think about the differences in the moment. They can take time later with their spectator perspective to analyze the differences. The ability to fluidly move from leader to manager and manager to leader with awareness and grace is obvious with exceptional leader-managers.

Leading is mostly about the future and doing right things. *Managing* is mostly about the present and doing things right.

He that would run a company on visible figures alone will in time have neither company or figures.

—W. Edwards Deming

Additional Thoughts

Consider the following ...

Does this book help you understand how I use the framework methodology and the ZL online tools to lead and manage Zynity? It should at least give you a general sense about how you lead and manage and make it easier to learn and apply more new things over time. You should, at a minimum, know we are structured, we have reasons for all we do, and we take pains to help others understand and engage with us at all levels of the organization.

With this full document, I meet with the other leaders and ask them to compare notes with me. Each of the other leaders and managers have their own *How You Lead and Manage* document. We collaborate, update, and refine our documents often. It only takes a few extra minutes a month and it's much better than just a journal tracking events and incidents chronologically.

The questions are the same for each of us: Are we on the same page? Do we agree with the general principles and objectives? What differences have we created during the last ninety days? What edits are needed? This makes it possible for us to review and determine which reports and metrics to look at to determine how we're doing.

There are fewer misunderstandings in the day-to-day activities when there is more structure. Few things get too far afield because we regularly update one another. This reduces the negative emotional cycles of distractions caused by misunderstandings and misfires. Chaos is not a good thing. Chaos doesn't promote creativity or allow for implementing innovation.

* * *

Positive and negative emotional cycles

* * *

Negative emotional cycles are those non-productive, wasted minutes being spent (involuntarily) thinking about past annoyances or anticipating potential future annoyances. These unnecessary emotional cycles occur more frequently in environments without definition and clarity. They eat up precious time and provide little value. They reduce an individual's energy. Each incident lends its own dysfunctional drama and erodes organizational effectiveness.

Positive emotional cycles are those productive moments or minutes being spent thinking about past successes and acknowledgements for work you've done well. These essential emotional cycles occur more frequently in environments with structure and a culture designed to encourage one another. These take little time and provide great value. They increase an individual's energy. Each incident builds its own momentum.

* * *

Structure and a positive culture

* * *

The structure provided by these documents and this process nurtures positive emotional cycles. Having your

163

leading and managing content in digital form and in this format changes individuals and the organization's culture. The examples we have are how we were changed with the use of browser-based CRM tools and project-management tools. The same dramatic evolution for leading and managing awaits those who adopt and adapt the *Framework for Leading*™ methodology and *Zynity Leadership*™ online tools.

Doing so makes it easier to adopt and adapt new leading and managing techniques and principles. With the digital leading and managing environment new things are easily added into the ongoing edits of these leading and managing tools. We now have a place, a consistent approach, and many others equally equipped to implement new things as a matter of course with forethought and specific expectations.

* * *

***Daily Dominant Themes* help you focus.**

* * *

I have what I call my **Daily Dominant Themes** to help me stay connected on a regular basis with all parts of our organization. These are the topics with which I'm mostly devoted on designated days. Flexibility is necessary but there is structure.

Monday – Operations and talent

Tuesday – Customers, clients, and alliances

Wednesday – Measurements and reporting

Thursday – Marketing, sales, and products

Friday – Preparation for next week and beyond

Saturday – Reflect, assess, listen to my thoughts

The themes above also direct a focus on the four **big parts**:
(1) Strategies
(2) Customers
(3) Managing team
(4) Measurements

The four big parts are presented at the start of this book and are presented in more detail in the *Framework for Leading*™ series of books. This published set of Daily Dominant Themes helps others arrange focused times more easily with me. If they have a topic they work to get it in the day I have set aside for the corresponding theme. It also informs everyone I am engaged with all parts of the organization and make time for all of them. They don't necessarily need me, but they need a person in my role connected with them. It also adds to the general sense of structure without rigidity.

The result is no big part gets ignored for too long. It's also appropriate to have two themes daily with one for morning and another for afternoon. This may be especially necessary for organizations implementing new major initiatives or during periods when extra efforts are required. Of course, these dominant-theme days and the themes can be edited and adjusted at any time. Also, it bears mentioning, the word *dominant* is used and not exclusive so there needs to be room for flexibility on any given day.

It is important for me to remain engaged with the major issues in each of the big parts with others on the leading and managing team. This allows me to have helpful in-depth discussions with the leaders and managers as we collaborate to establish proper principles and guidelines. This demonstrates I respect all they do to innovate within the big picture. It makes it easier for them to implement all the details exceptionally. It's how we put the big issues and the hard ones at the front of our deliverables and activities lists even when it isn't fun.

I often try to say the same thing in different ways in more than one place in a book. I haven't deliberately repeated a section word for word until now. I don't want anyone to miss it if possible. If it stuck out and remained with you from the first time, this refresher won't hurt. The following paragraph bears repeating.

Experience and knowledge

Experience is the best teacher. Knowledge is power. These two statements are acknowledged as truths by almost everyone. I agree. However, when we say them, we also include the qualifiers, even if unspoken, that these truths are very dependent on the individual. If we don't actively and deliberately learn from the experiences we have, then we may not learn all we should. If we don't use and apply the knowledge we accumulate correctly and fully, then the impact of its power is diminished. Experience can be the best teacher. Knowledge provides the potential for great power. This book and its related materials and activities are designed to help us intentionally *learn* from our experiences and *apply* what we know for its maximum impact.

Boards are essential.

Creating a board is important for most organizations as they begin to grow to certain size. The size varies based on the type of business.

Boards serve a much different purpose in a formal sense than do outside professionals such as accountants and lawyers. Boards focus on governance, which is quite different than operational excellence. The general definition of corporate governance is usually something like the following:

> The framework of rules, principles, and practices through which a board of directors, or board of advisors ensure accountability, fairness, and transparency in an organization's relationship with all its stakeholders. Stakeholders includes financiers, customers, management, employees, government, and the community they serve.

Limited Liability Corporations should have a very well defined and focused board of advisors. They are designated as advisors as they have much less legal binding and responsibility than the board of directors in a corporation.

This topic is presented here as a reminder. There are many organizations with expertise in helping organizations establish their boards. Find one of these experts and begin preparing so you know when and how to establish your own board.

I admire and respect all who lead, manage, and grow organizations. I know this will help you and those with whom you work improve your parts of the world daily. Just get started. Ignition! The value of doing this will become obvious in a very short while. You will have lots of help from the others. Some will find this very easy to do and make it easier for everyone. And, as you now suspect … it is never finished. Each one of you TIs working together will continue making the structure serve you all better.

The call to action is this:

Begin immediately writing your own document describing how you lead and manage your organization or your part of an organization. It should include most, if not all, of the above topics in the outline provided above.

Once the writing begins, engage others in the process to encourage and provide input to this document. In this process, you'll identify and clarify issues and opportunities for your organization to address in its ongoing deliberate need to improve. You'll be much more organized in how you lead and manage.

Transform with Harmony

Connected and working together better

The process of implementing the *Framework for Leading*™ methodology in your organization will transform the individuals and the organization. Getting the various teams in your organization connected with the sharing of their Weekly DnAs™ will remove walls, build bridges, and establish an open culture allowing everyone to work together better and pull in the same direction. Having the purpose, vision, mission, and core values woven throughout the entire operating fabric of your organization will transform the organization and everyone in it.

The methodology establishes a shared and broad perspective about all parts of the organization. This helps each person maintain focus on the right issues at all times in the right context. Each person will:

- Share an accurate view of the organization.
- Build and receive trust.
- Understand how it all works together.
- Anticipate needs for next stages in advance of implementing them.

The above allows for better collaboration and community. The result is everyone will …

work together in harmony!

The Assessment

Are the leading and managing capabilities all you need them to be in your organization?

Are you open to learning more about this?

The following brief assessment, which can also be accessed at www.Zynity.com, will let you know how well *you* think you're doing on each item. Once at the home page, click on **The Assessment** link and it'll guide you through a process with instructions on how to use the assessment tool.

The Assessment allows you to gain more insight about your organization and how well it currently implements these four top-level big parts:

- Strategies
- Customers
- Managing team
- Measurements

Assess yourself and your managing team: (Rate each one from zero to ten, with ten being highest)

The assessment questions are below: Read through them and think about your current situation. Then go to the website and begin the process of implementing a framework for leading and managing in your organization.

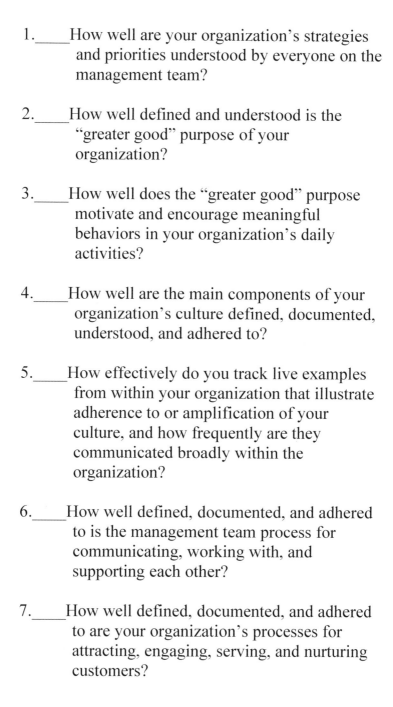

1.____How well are your organization's strategies and priorities understood by everyone on the management team?

2.____How well defined and understood is the "greater good" purpose of your organization?

3.____How well does the "greater good" purpose motivate and encourage meaningful behaviors in your organization's daily activities?

4.____How well are the main components of your organization's culture defined, documented, understood, and adhered to?

5.____How effectively do you track live examples from within your organization that illustrate adherence to or amplification of your culture, and how frequently are they communicated broadly within the organization?

6.____How well defined, documented, and adhered to is the management team process for communicating, working with, and supporting each other?

7.____How well defined, documented, and adhered to are your organization's processes for attracting, engaging, serving, and nurturing customers?

171

8.____Do you have written standards for the
development and use of reports?

9.____How effective is your report-review process
for ensuring the correct reports are created
and effectively used across the organization?

Basic instructions for use:

Step 1: Principal Leaders (PLs) should answer these
questions on their own, with no one else aware
of their answers until the right time to share
them.

Step 2: PLs should have their management team answer
these questions on their own. Their individual
answers may be kept anonymous but presented
as group averages publicly.

Step 3: PLs should meet with the group to discuss
average ratings for each topic.

Step 4: PLs may meet with each one separately to get
insights about how to improve.

Step 5: PLs should commit to implementing the
Framework for Leading™ concepts and the
Zynity Leadership™ (ZL) online tools. Continue
taking the assessment every quarter by going
through steps 1–4 above to track and celebrate
progress.

A combined low rating for any category could indicate
that there are opportunities for increased understanding
and more effective communication. Key: assess and

track ratings over time. There will likely be up and down ratings. The path to success is not usually a straight line.

Expected results:

Working to make the ratings better over time is a good way to keep score of your organization's progress. Your Key Performance Metrics (KPMs) will get better if you improve the environment in which they are created. Improving the environment entails improving the foundation upon which it is built. A key strength of the foundation is its organized leadership-and-management framework.

If the *Zynity Leadership*™ (ZL) online tools and concepts are properly used, the ratings for each of these questions will increase quarter after quarter. The goal is to get the ratings nearer to ten for all respondents in the organization. This will indicate that a top-level leadership-and-management system is in place and having a significant impact. All those who do this will have a decided advantage in their goal of building a thriving organization.

Leading and managing is a team effort. Get you and your team working together building your own framework in only one hour a week. You will notice many worthwhile changes within a short time. You will be motivated to continue evolving by the ongoing improvements you experience. In a short time, you will be a whole new team. No one will complain about the process or the outcomes.

Using the *Framework for Leading*™ methodology

Teaching materials are available to companies wanting to implement this on their own or with the help of a *Zynity Leadership*™ Certified Coach. Please connect with us at the following website and go to the link at *Coaches* at the home page:

<u>www.Zynity.com</u>

Ask for information via chat or email or call the telephone number provided.

Certified Coaches

Certified Coaches are individuals who help organizations implement and use the *Framework for Leading*™ methodology and *Zynity Leadership*™ (ZL) online tools. They're listed on Zynity's website, so organizations can reach out to them when they need help in implementing the methodology.

Individuals who would like to become certified as coaches are invited to visit the website and follow the path indicated to apply for certification. On the website, you will receive directions regarding how to obtain thorough training on the methodology, concept, and practical implementation of the *Zynity Leadership*™ (ZL) online tools. You will have access to the necessary set of materials and be included in the referral network for coaching/consulting opportunities.

If you would like to apply to become a Certified Coach, please go to the website and follow the instructions, or email us at:

Coaches@Zynity.com

It's a solution...

to define and clarify your leadership!

What does it accomplish?

Framework → Structure

Structure → Effectiveness

Effectiveness → Growth and Profitability

How do you make it work for you?

Your* 'How I Lead and Manage' *document

Combined with ...

***Framework for Leading*™ methodology**

Combined with ...

***Zynity Leadership*™ (ZL) online tools**

Combined with ...

ZL *Certified Coaches* network

Do you need this?

If you are asked ...

> How do you keep everyone focused on the right issues at the right time?
>
> Is everyone properly customer focused?
>
> Does everyone use our reporting effectively?
>
> How easily does your organization innovate?
>
> How do you lead and manage your organization?

Is there an opportunity to improve your answers to these questions?

This book presents the plan and a process.

Theme: Clear and defined leadership is essential.

The 5 musts for Leading and Managing

Continually refine each one.

(1) Clarify and express how you lead and manage
(so, others can engage correctly and effectively)
   a. Philosophy about leading and managing
   b. Clarify what the organization contributes
   c. Your organization
   d. Use of resources
   e. Development of individuals

(2) Connect and align the team
(so, they work together more efficiently and effectively)
   a. Know what others are doing
   b. Reduce email clutter and save time
   c. Keep exchanges in a concise journal
   d. Improve communicating skills and habits
   e. Keep everyone on the same page

(3) Develop and implement key strategies
(so, the business has directional momentum)
   a. Identify needed fixes and positive opportunities
   b. Clarify fixes and opportunities
   c. Assess value of each one
   d. Schedule the right sequence
   e. Execute with excellence

(4) Be completely customer focused
(so, everyone knows how they add to serving customers)
a. Who are the customers and/or clients?
b. Their view of the organization
c. Their expectations in the relationship
d. Express how our operations serve them
e. Measure our customer focus effectiveness

(5) Measure and manage the right things
(so, all resources create great results)
a. Budgets and plans
b. Key Performance Metrics (KPMs)
c. Financial reports (P&L, BS, CF)
d. Operating reports
e. Assess report use and impact regularly

Acknowledgments

It is a special honor to thank Robert H. Breinholt, PhD, a longtime professor at The Wharton School, University of Pennsylvania, and the University of Utah. Dr. Breinholt was one of my spectacular professors during my time at Wharton. He was also my first business partner. We developed and conducted leadership and management seminars throughout the United States during the seventies. That experience and the relationship that grew between us have been invaluable throughout my life.

He earned his master's degree in business administration (MBA) from Harvard Business School and his PhD in industrial psychology at Stanford University. He was one of the youngest professors at Wharton when I first met him. His intellect was gargantuan, his heart without limit, and his humor is still the most favored in my life. For an eight-year period, we shared over a hundred filled days each year on the road, conducting seminars. It was a great joy to be around him.

Thank you, Bob. You're gone from this earth, but your many contributions and inspiration live on. May this book be worthy of you and all that you worked so hard to instill in me and others as you exemplified in full force the meaning of a caring and committed professor. I miss you and am much less without you.

Encouragers

... without whom this would not be

I appreciate very much the following individuals who have provided specific and wonderful suggestions to make this book better: Jason Britt; Keith Burns; Stephen Callahan; Janet M. Canova; Dennis Eastham; Lawrence J. Genalo, Jr.; Rick Gibson; Wayne R. Haggstrom; Kenneth W. (Ken) Hein; Maryjo Kulp; Jim Laird; James A. (Jim) Miller; Mark R. Miller, Terry Mullane; Kent Petzold; Andrew Pinch; Ron Sciarro; Wayne B. (Smitty) Smith; Katherine Trontell; Fred Weling, PhD; Laura Whitson; and Michael Wilmet.

My encouragers, friends, and associates who have selflessly participated in improving the methodology, online tools, and the book series are: David B. Abright; Susan Anderson; Tom Anton, PGA professional; David Auterson; Pamela Barker; Nelson Baxley; James S. Berry, PhD; Chris Black; Anne Marie Blankenship; John Bower; Tom Bradburn; Robert H. Breinholt, PhD; Jason Britt; Keith Burns; Stephen Callahan; Janet M. Canova; Joel Cash; Chris Cole; Cary C. Covert; Robby Culbreath; Dennis Eastham; Adriana Enloe; Mike Ennis; Scot Foss; David Fried; Rick Gibson; Lawrence J. Genalo, Jr.; Allen Gjersvig; Jeremy Goodman, Esq.; Hayford Gyampoh; Wayne R. Haggstrom; Patrick Harter; Kenneth W. (Ken) Hein; Richard A. Herzog; Malcolm Hilcove; Rick Hoefert; Al Hubbard; Lawrence A. Husick, Esq.; Dewey James; Donna James; James; Vanessa Joaquim; Jon Kaplan; Steve Katz; Tara Kellerhals; Glen Kerby; H. William Knapp; Gene Konstant; Maryjo Kulp; Michael

181

T. Kutzman, Esq.; Jim Laird; Jennifer Levine; Allen Lorenzi; Douglas Marshall; Rick Marshall; Patrick McCalla; Don McCormick; Bill F. Miller; James A. (Jim) Miller; Mark R. Miller; Mike Mitchell; Joseph Morehouse; Scott Morehouse; Terry Mullane; Will Neitzke; Jim Nissen, Sr.; Jim O'Connor; Timothy Olp; Ralph Palmen; Larry Parsons; Paul Palmer; Deborah Peck, PhD; Cary Peters; Scott A. Peters; Kent Petzold; Andrew Pinch; Nick Puente; JoAn Risdon; Ron Sciarro; Gary G. Small; Wayne B. (Smitty) Smith; Dan F. Spencer; Brent Spore; Mike Stowell; Daniel Stringer; Jeff Struble; Eric Taylor; Jami Throne; Katherine Trontell; Donna Rae Upshaw; Richard E. Upshaw (F&B); Lisa Villaluna; Fred Weling, PhD; Laura Whitson; Don Wiest; Brandon Willey; Craig Williamson; Michael Wilmet; and Kent Wilson. Quite a village!

My children, Laura, Ryan, and Stephen, have given much and are great encouragers. I'm especially thankful to my wife, Janet, for the support, input, and commitment to our personal lives and professional careers. She is the most influential and patient teacher in my life. She is my most ardent supporter and sincerest critic in the very best sense. Much of this foundational thinking has come from questions and insights she shared as we partnered during our entrepreneurial ventures.

Thank you all for caring, your understanding, and encouragement. I'm very hopeful this book and its related materials bring happiness and value to you and many others.

The Author

Dwaine Canova is an international entrepreneur who started and grew his own companies and is now helping others grow theirs. Clients of his companies included IBM, Sun Microsystems, Pacific Bell, Qwest, Bell South, JC Penney, Sears, NTT (Japan's largest telephone company), Godiva, and hundreds of other international and regional companies.

In this series of practical books, he unveils a methodology being used by organizations of every type and size to improve how individuals work together. He has been the founder of three companies; all became notable in their fields He has served as CEO of two others and COO of two additional companies. He built one company from a staff of one to more than three thousand employees, operating in five countries with dozens of billion-dollars, multinational companies as clients and alliance partners. He has helped in the development and growth of many other organizations.

Mr. Canova is the CEO of Zynity, LLC, the developer and provider of the online SaaS (Software-as-a-Service) tools to help management teams perform their day-to-day activities more effectively. He is also the CEO of Framework for Leading Institute, LLC, an organization conducting education and research in leadership.

He has spoken around the world on leadership development and the *why* and *how* of leveraging information to improve customer acquisition, retention, and service. Mr. Canova's speech to the Stanford Alumni

Association is sold as part of the association's video series entitled "Executive Briefings." The title of the video is *Customer Focused Companies: Using Integrated Marketing Practices to Increase Profitability.* He served for two years as an instructor in the Academic Computer Center at the United States Military Academy at West Point.

Mr. Canova is the author of the *A Framework for Leading*™ series and *Overcoming the Four Deceptions in Career Relationships,* a motivational book presenting his experiences and observations on interpersonal communication in organizations. It provides understanding and techniques designed to help individuals work more effectively together.

He has an MBA from The Wharton School, University of Pennsylvania, where he was also a teaching fellow, as well as a BS in agronomy from California State University, Fresno.

Contact Dwaine

dwaine@DwaineCanova.com

To get the latest *A Framework for Leading*™ updates,

visit: ZynityLeader.com

Dwaine speaks frequently on many topics including: top-level leadership and management, *A Framework for Leading*™, emerging growth companies, leadership, management, mentoring, coaching, and entrepreneurship. He provides full-day, half-day, or keynote versions on these topics. If you want to find out more, please visit his speaking page at:

DwaineCanova.com/speaking

You can also connect with Dwaine at:

Blog: DwaineCanova.com

Twitter: twitter.com/DwaineCanova

Facebook: facebook.com/dwainecanova

Blog: ZynityLeader.com

Twitter: twitter.com/ZynityLeader

Dwaine's mission: Serving* leaders and managers

*Serving is helping, responding, anticipating, and encouraging with full attention to another's best interests.

Also, by Dwaine Canova:

Overcoming the Four Deceptions:
In Career Relationships

A Framework for Leading™ Series

Improve leading and managing in your organization.

Books:
1 – A Framework for Leading™***:***
Simple – Easy – Effective
(Building a Foundation)

2 – A Framework for Leading™***:***
The Top Level
(Elevate Your View)

3 – A Framework for Leading™***:***
Advantages
(A Managing Methodology for Leaders)

4 – A Framework for Leading™***:***
Expectations and Outcomes
(Anticipate and Innovate)

5 – A Framework for Leading™***:***
Connect and Align
(Communicating in High-Performance Organizations)

6 – A Framework for Leading™***:***
Strategic Initiatives
(Create, Prioritize, and Execute Strategies)

More books are coming in this series …

Other books being prepared for this series:

Available 2018
7 – A Framework for Leading™:
Customers and Clients
(Structure to Attract, Engage, and Serve)

This book will present how the *Framework for Leading™* methodology enhances the organization's ability to attract, engage, and serve its customers. The concepts, principles, and tools guide the development and processes necessary for the organization to structure itself explicitly to be operationally customer focused.

Available 2018
8 – A Framework for Leading™:
Measurements
(Measuring and Managing the Right Things)

This book will present how the *Framework for Leading™* methodology enhances identification, measurement, and management of the right things within an organization. The concepts, principles, and tools help focus individuals in organizations on the right issues at the right times. This makes it easier to work together better and perform at their highest levels.

Available 2018
9 – A Framework for Leading™:
The Coaching Role
(Learning Together to Accelerate Development)

This book will present how a ZL Certified Coach helps organizations implement the *Framework for Leading™*

methodology. They help install the processes, attitudes, and behaviors required for a leading and managing team to work together more effectively. The process presented in this book includes development of individuals as well as adding structure for the organization's, attitudes, and behaviors required for a leading and managing team to work together more effectively. The process includes development of individuals as well as adding leadership definition and clarity for the organization.

For more information, address requests to:

books@DwaineCanova.com

books@ZynityLeader.com

A Framework for Leading™:
A Series of Books

Improve leadership and management in your organization.

by
Dwaine Canova

Objective: Improve the leadership and management capabilities, capacities, and outcomes in small and midsize businesses (SMBs).

Symptoms: Few organizations perform at their desired level. Many struggle and are characterized by poor communication, chaos, and anemic growth. Of the 100 million American workers, **50** percent are not engaged and inspired, **20** percent are actively disengaged, and only **30** percent are engaged[1]. **Fifty-five** percent of small and midsize businesses fail before the end of their fifth year; the number jumps to **70** percent by year ten[2]. **Seventy-five** percent of venture-capital-funded companies don't make a return for their investors[3].

Problems: Leading and managing organizations is difficult. Building the new capabilities needed for growth isn't easy while coping with the demands of daily operations. Too much time spent on daily hot issues traps management into ongoing firefighting mode. The result is there is little time available to invest in a leadership and management structure. Leadership by the seat of the pants happening on the fly is cause for alarm.

Solution: Design and Implement a holistic approach to leading and managing your organization. Being organized with what you already know and do makes leading easier, more efficient, and more effective. Implement this simple and easy-to-use leadership and management structure. This will be your foundation for profitable and stable growth.

Results: With this solution, organizations can expect accelerated growth, higher margins, fewer failures, and more successes through increased productivity and performance. The new work environment enhances individual engagement and reduces stress. Individuals become more collaborative and interdependent.

Audience: Individuals in organizations dedicated to improving their leadership and management capabilities, capacities, and outcomes.

Books: Individual books in the series don't need to be read in a specific order. It's expected readers will be drawn to each books' subtitle and topics suiting their needs and interests at the moment. Each one can set his or her own reading sequences to match their individual needs. The first four volumes are intended to introduce the basic concepts, with discussions about applying the framework methodology. Ongoing use of each book in the series as a reference and resource is expected.

Much of the teaching in the books is centered around refining how you apply the knowledge and experience you already have. It also makes it easier to adopt and incorporate your new learnings.

The books will be most effective if the reading is done while applying the framework concepts using the *Zynity Leadership*™ (ZL) online tools. In this way, the learning evolves in a manner and pace to suit the reader/user. There is overlap and repetition of some themes among the books to reinforce and expand certain concepts.

This form of "street" learning and applying emphasizes your daily experiences are the primary opportunity and source for learning. The objective is to be the Practical Elite™ who correctly apply what they learn and not the academic elite. The value of learning here is not to pass a test. It's to accelerate the growth and successes of individuals and organizations.

The framework methodology guides you with practical concepts, principles, and use of online tools. Leadership is more than solving problems. It's also about preventing problems and creating opportunities. The *Framework for Leading*™ methodology gets leaders out of the firefighting mode and they become better at implementing new opportunities as needed.

[1] Gallup Research.
http://www.gallup.com/topic/employee_engagement.aspx

[2] United States Small Business Administration.
http://www.isbdc.org/small-business-failure-rates-causes/
http://www.statisticbrain.com/startup-failure-by-industry/

[3] Shikhar Ghosh, a senior lecturer at Harvard Business School.
http://www.wsj.com/articles/SB1000087239639044372020457800498 04
76429190

Made in the USA
Middletown, DE
21 September 2021

48819850R00110